Boy U

Dennis Nilsen: The Story of a Serial Killer

by Rhiannon D'Averc

Prologue: The Drowning Boy

The boy stands and stares out at the sea. The roiling, hissing mass of waves seems to call out to him, beckoning him in closer. He had been walking to Inverallochy, but now there is something in the waves that he cannot ignore. It is big, and powerful, and he cannot look away.

Pushed by a sudden impulse, he bends down and takes off first his shoes, then his socks. The miserable feeling that he has been fighting off all morning is amplified by the sound of the waves, but somehow made better, also. There is something out there that he must go to find. Something that resonates deep within his soul and fits neatly.

He walks into the swell, first feeling the familiar, freezing shock of the water hitting his bare feet, and then absorbing it. He needs more. He walks forward a few more steps, until the water is up to his knees.

The boy is wearing short trousers, and if he goes home with them dripping wet, perhaps he will be in trouble with Granny. For now, he doesn't care. He walks forward further still, stepping and stepping until the green-blue water is whirling around his waist. There is something calming in it, the feel of the salty sea lapping his skin, the way it has done time and time again since he was so young he can no longer remember it. He briefly thinks about feeling it all over his skin, on every part of him.

The boy looks around. There is another, older boy, perhaps a teenager, poking at the shore with a stick a little further along. He is the only intruder on this stretch of sand.

The boy walks on confidently into the waves. All of a sudden, the flooring of soft sand is gone and he realises he is being swept away, head fully under the water and all the world a haze of green and grey now. The current is taking him, and the spell it cast over him is broken; he kicks out, grabs a lungful of air and yells, waving his arms and desperately reaching for a help which is not yet there.

Then he is under the water again – unable to gasp for a breath, taking in water instead, hearing a buzzing in his head. This is where Grandad is, he remembers. This is where Grandad went the last time I saw him before he was dead. For a still, calm moment he feels sure that Grandad will come to rescue him, plucking him out of the green weight of the waves that sits now on his shoulders, holding him in his strong arms. It feels like a dream. Somewhere, someone is shouting, but the voice is so far away and so drowsy that he cannot hold onto it. More – he does not want to.

At first, he becomes aware of the cold, then it is gone; and then a slow warmth that must have been the sun. The boy vomits and gasps, continuing to try to throw up water even when it is all out of him, his whole body heaving and shuddering under the weight of the sea that now prowls restlessly a little distance away.

There is blue sky; there is air; there is a breeze playfully running over his naked body. There is safety. To the side he sees his clothes, spread out as if to dry in the sun. There is a pressure still, as if the waves hang over his head, even though he sees wisps of clouds hanging in the blue sky. He closes his eyes again, ready to dry out in the sun just like his clothes.

When the boy wakes next, he knows that he is really awake. The dry sand underneath his bare back is comforting somehow, a familiar touch learned in years of life alongside the sea. His throat is dry and raspy, and from the height of the sun alone he knows that it is time to get up and go home.

He reaches with small hands to cover his nakedness, a modesty belied by all this time he has spent sleeping, open to the world. There is something on his thigh and stomach – a white sticky mess – something that could not have been there before he went in the water. It would have washed away. He frowns, thinks of seagulls soaring over his prone body, and scrubs it off with the sand.

The boy's clothes are still damp, but he puts them on, feeling the heat of the sun and hoping it will dry them out. He cautiously peers around through the long grasses, but no one is there. Not even the boy who must have saved him. Not his Grandad, who he saw under the sea. Only he remains to stalk this stretch of lonely sand.

He sighs, squares his shoulders. At home, he knows, a row awaits over where he has been and what he has done. His mother and grandmother will scold him over the state of his clothes. Leaving the grumbling sea behind, knowing now that it cannot claim him yet, he takes the long walk home.

Chapter One

The man relaxes against the bar in a pub in the West End, holding a pint in one hand while the other rests nonchalantly on the worn wood. He gazes around the room somewhat dispassionately, allowing his eyes to rest on someone at the other end of the bar for long enough to invite approach without seeming desperate.

She doesn't seem to get it. A small flare of doubt: after all, he's out of practice.

No, he reminds himself. He's a red-blooded male, a fully-fledged bisexual. Just because he's been with men for the most part doesn't mean he can't pick up a girl once in a while.

She is blonde, which pleases him. It reminds him of Twink, who is no longer waiting for him back at the house. Maybe he can replace one kind of thing with another, prove that he's still got it.

He sidles over to her, slides his drink across the bar. She looks up a little nervously and smiles.

"Good evenin', gorgeous," he says, his Scottish brogue just thick enough to be attractive.

"Hi," she says, beaming at the compliment. There's a European turn to her accent. "What's your name?"

He leans back a little, as if making a big pronouncement. "Everyone calls me Des," he says, with a flourish. "What about you, my lovely?"

"Elizabeth," she tells him, and then, as if the two things go together, "I'm an au pair."

Des raises his eyebrows. He's heard a bit about au pairs. "Is that right?" he asks, with a little chuckle. She laughs, too. Somehow, he just knows they're going to get along famously.

Later, when they are back in the house on Melrose Avenue together, and she has gone to sleep, he stares up at the ceiling. The same ceiling that he looked at every night for the last two years, but the difference was that Twinkle was always here then.

Des had to push the two beds together before she came in the room, forming the pretence of a single bed. The kind of bed a single man might have ready and waiting for his conquests. He supposes he is a single man, now. Elizabeth was a bit of fun, but she was hardly material for keeping around.

He can't sleep. Frankly, he was pretty impressed with himself for managing to get off with her, but now that the buzz is fading it's all becoming a little too real. Des prefers things to have more of a cinematic feel to them. He sighs, slides out from the covers, and paces through to the living room.

Bleep, his black and white mongrel bitch, jumps up and clatters over to him on affectionate paws as he sits heavily on the sofa. She rests her head on his knee and he smiles. Bleep would never abandon him, that much was for certain. She might only be a dog, but she would never abandon him.

Not like Twinkle. David. No use in cute pet names now, now that David was swanning around the West Country with some antiques dealer he had met in Soho. The stupid little poof.

He'd had it all with Des, all given him on a platter. Des hadn't minded when he went off to Soho and brought back whoever he wanted. Well, at least except for the times when stuff got nicked. That was going too far. But Des hadn't complained about the other times. Hadn't forced himself on him except when they were both up for it. Hadn't even turned his nose up when this hairy, skin and bone, effeminate little Welshman had come strolling into the Champion pub and met him for the first time.

He'd paid for everything. The furniture around him, the food he ate, the dog. They'd found the cat together and named it Deedee – for Dennis and David. He had paid for the alcohol, provided the music.

Even the flat was paid for with Des' money – well, no, accurately it was paid for with his father's money. When Olav Moksheim – the mockery of a father who had never even bothered to stick around for his son or give him a real last name – had passed away, he'd left a princely sum of £1,400 to what turned out to be just one of his many children.

Moksheim. What a joke. All his life he'd been brought up a Nilsen, and now over 29 years later to find out there wasn't such a thing. What was he now, eh? It had been two years and he still felt like he must be a Nilsen. Even if the name was fake, given to his mother as a spiteful wedding present that later allowed him to start a new family, it was the realest thing Des had. So, it stuck.

Des rolls his eyes at himself and forces himself up. The au pair is still in the bedroom. Surely, she'll be game for one more round. That ought to shake him out of this mess.

After she leaves in the morning, Des sits in the garden with Bleep and stares angrily into the pond. The pond he had put in himself, with Twinkle's help. That was the insult of it, the real kick.

Bleep is nervous and growling, low in her throat. Des soothes her with one hand across the top of her head, stroking softly.

"Enough of that, Bleep," he says. "You stay quiet now."

She settles down a little, though she still looks at the pond with the white of her eyes showing.

Des knows how she feels. That was the last straw, really it was. Coming home and finding those puppies drowned, and Twinkle sitting there out of his head in the living room, not even noticing they were missing. Des had yelled at him that night, yelled at him like he never had before. Given the amount of times he had yelled, that was saying something. He'd called him things like stupid poof and dumb fag and got right up in his face. He had started planning internally about how he would get rid of Twinkle, psyching himself up to it. He had never really managed to get there.

That was two weeks ago, and Twinkle had gone and found someone else to run off with.

"Discarded like yesterday's trash, girl," Des says quietly, staring into the pond and stroking Bleep's fur. "Just the two of us now, and that cat. Got to stick together from now on."

Bleep whimpers, a soft grief in the back of her throat. All of the puppies are gone now, sold off or dead. She knows what it's like to have her heart ripped out. Des knows what it's like to be left alone, now, too.

It's not enough anymore, picking up these men in pubs. Des still goes through the motions all the same, but none of them stay for long. He knows his chance for domestic bliss has long since slipped away. Anyway, it's all the same to him. He's got a way to get his own release, no need for anyone else.

He lays back on his bed, ready to indulge. It has been the same since his army days, when he first discovered the image of himself in a full-length mirror, and he always has his imagination. He can think back to those images and use them again whenever he wants.

He strips himself fully, feeling the vulnerability of the position. He settles back in a relaxed state, as if he is unconscious or even dead. He imagines himself as a hairless youth, all shining young flesh and smoothness. He thinks back to the body he had seen in the mirror, when he angled it to hide his own face and allow his imagination to create someone else. Then, he imagines himself, too, as a dirty old man, a leering pervert who comes across this defenceless young man.

As the old man has his way with the prone body, doing whatever he wants to it without any fear of being stopped, he is in total control. When the old man finds his release, Des does, too.

When it is all over he is himself again, just one person: Dennis Nilsen. The old man and the youth store themselves away in his mind for a later date, and he opens the door to let Bleep in, deciding to sleep off his hangover.

Chapter Two

The crippling loneliness gets darker and darker as the year goes on. Worst of all is Christmas time. Des sits with Bleep and Deedee and tries to imagine a life where this wasn't how it always had to be. A life where he could actually have settled down with someone and found some semblance of domestic bliss.

He isn't stupid. He knows that Twinkle was only with him for the security of it all. There wasn't any romance between them, certainly not a good fuck. When they talked, it was Des yelling, and Twinkle cowering or taking it on the chin placidly. There had never been any reason for him to stay for long.

There have been a few others since Twinkle left, but they all left, one way or another. It seems as though no one can stand to be around him for long.

Now, Des is about to ring in 1979 alone. He hates it. He can't stand it. The loneliness is like an oppressive force now, crushing him with a long and unbearable pain. He is even starting to feel a little detached, going through life as if it is a series of motions only. No one is even paying attention to him anymore.

Bleep is good company, but not enough for the only company. It's New Year's Eve, for Christ's sake. Time to get out of here and find some fun.

He heads out, but everywhere is quiet. People are finding fun in their own homes, gathering together with family and friends. He's had enough of this. Then at last it looks like the Cricklewood Arms is livelier than all of the rest: not his usual kind of haunt, full of Irish Republicans for the most part, but it'll do. Any port in a storm.

Des settles in at the bar. He tries not to think about getting passed over for a promotion yet again, or how his union activity doesn't seem to be making any difference. He tries not to think about the cold, empty flat. He tries not to think about the puppies buried in the garden, or the family back home in Scotland who he hasn't spoken to in years.

He tries not to think about anything, and looks at the boy leaning up against the bar a short distance away.

Pint of Guinness in hand, Des walks over to the smaller boy, casting a gaze over his curly brown hair, his young features, the gentle innocence of him.

"Des," he says by way of introduction, holding out a hand.

The boy goes to shake it instinctively. He has rough hands, despite his age. Des pegs him as a teen, though he's in here drinking sure enough. Must be at least eighteen, then.

"Stephen," the boy says, and now the two of them have a reason to go on talking.

It turns out the boy is Southern Irish, down in the city for some exploration, talking about things like he's a man when he clearly isn't. Des likes that about him. The cocksureness of it combined with a shyness hidden behind the exterior, a shyness that he might be caught out. They knock back drink after drink at the bar together, until it finally comes closing time.

Closing time on New Year's. Not worth thinking about, going home alone. If he drank himself to death alone tonight, Des knows with a certainty, no one would find his body until he was stinking and rotten and attracting flies. Probably only then because people in the other flats would complain of the smell.

So, he invites young Steve back with him and they go for another drink in the flat. Some rum, some vodka, some more beer.

What do they talk about? Des barely knows the answer himself once they leave the pub, but all of it is revolutionary. All of it would set the world on fire if someone else heard it. They talk about the working class and the government and the trade unions and the workforce. The boy nods his head a lot more the drunker he gets.

Eventually, they're both so drunk they can't even do that. Des suggests they go to sleep and the boy nods again. They both undress, fumbling with drunk, awkward hands, the boy not even sober enough to feel bashful as he kicks his trousers over into the corner of the room. Des thinks, looking at him, that maybe the boy isn't quite eighteen after all.

They get under the covers, shivering a little when cold skin touches by accident, settling their spinning heads against pillows that will be spinning a lot more in the morning.

When Stephen is asleep, Des wakes up and looks at him, and that feeling of loneliness descends again. It is a crushing despair. He is all alone, and in the morning, what then? This boy will leave, probably at the first chance he gets. He'll be just another ship passing in the night, another male floating away from him, no desire to stay.

Suddenly, Des is desperate for him to stay. He is driven almost to tears by it. He wants it more than anything he can think of right then. He can't spend another night alone, not like this, not at New Year's. This is a time for fresh starts, not for sinking back into that same old black pit, alone again.

If only there was a way to make him stay.

He pulls the blanket down over both of them, around halfway, so he can admire Stephen's body and his own. The fire has been on all night, so the small flat is warm enough. Idly, he sits and traces shapes and lines over the skin of Stephen's back, admiring how smooth and unmarked it is. He stays that way for hours, basking in it, enjoying every part of Stephen that he can see.

Then it is the morning. Stephen will be going soon.

Des feels his heart pounding suddenly, and arousal stirring. It brings a quick heat that makes him sweat, staring at this unconscious young body, feeling his own body respond. They didn't do anything last night. This body, though. It calls to him.

He glances over at the floor and sees his tie lying there, pooled on top of his other clothes. He stares at it for a little while, sweating, nervous, feeling an excited energy which has never been so strong before. He reaches out and pulls the tie over.

Stephen has to stay for the New Year. He has to, whether he wants to or not. Des won't be alone again.

He slips the tie over Stephen's neck, straddles him, and pulls it hard. Stephen wakes up almost immediately, confused, still half-drunk and half-asleep.

"What the -" he gets out, but Des pulls tighter and cuts him off. Stephen struggles and they roll together, off the bed and onto the floor, but Des has the upper hand. Stephen uses his feet desperately to push, trying to move his body further away, but Des is like a dog with a rat now. He knows he only has to hang on the longest, nothing more.

The coffee table goes over. The glasses from last night. The ashtray goes. An almighty mess and clatter, and Stephen's head is up against the wall, and he has nowhere left to go. He struggles and struggles for a half-minute more, getting weaker all the time. Finally, he goes limp, and Des figures it is done.

He stands up, and lets go of the tie. He can feel himself trembling, the exertion and the tension taking away his core. It's all he can do to get his breathing under control, but then he hears a noise and realises that Stephen is breathing again too. Raspy, short, hard breaths. The breaths of someone trying to fight back to life. Well, that won't do at all.

But what next? The tie didn't work. Des thinks for a moment and goes to the kitchen, then pulls out a bucket and fills it with water. That ought to do the job. Returning to Stephen, Des picks him up and drapes his limp body over a dining chair, the bucket of water close by. Now it's just an easy bit of work to move his head into the bucket and hold it there, under the water. Water splashes up and over the carpet but there is no more struggle. No more movement. Just a few bubbles, and it is done.

It is done.

Des looks at him for a moment, his still form, head still under the water. This body is his now. This body has to stay.

He lifts the body up and sets it comfortably in the chair, the head lolling back. Water drips from the curls of hair down onto the carpet.

Des stares for a while, trying to get his thoughts in order. He wants to think clearly about what he has done, but it is hard to get a grasp on things. *I strangled him nearly to death. I put his head in water deliberately. I drowned him. I killed him. He is dead,* he thinks.

He is still shaking, even harder now. He has killed someone. He has taken this boy's life and turned him into a body only.

He thinks about Stephen's family – his mother and father. His siblings, perhaps. His friends. He thinks about the police. He thinks about prison and how many years you get for murder. He thinks about what you do with dead bodies and how to get rid of evidence. He thinks about the deaths he saw while he was in the army and how nobody cared at all if you killed someone there. He thinks about the death in his family, his dead grandfather. He thinks about masturbating in front of the mirror and pretending to be dead himself. He thinks about the old man and the powerless youth. He thinks about going to prison for a very long time. He thinks about the mess they have made in the room. He thinks about the coffee table and the glasses and the bucket of water and the water on the carpet. He thinks about the noise. He thinks about the sun, rising soon. He thinks about being carted out in handcuffs. He thinks about going to work. He thinks about Stephen's family. He thinks about the body.

Finally, he gets up and does something. He makes a cup of coffee and drinks it, smokes a cigarette, then another. He decides that he will continue to smoke until the shaking stops.

He clears up the mess, the glasses and the coffee table, working around the body of the dead youth. Bleep wanders in from the garden and starts to sniff around; he can't have that.

"Fuck off, Bleep," he says, grabbing her by the scruff of the neck and pushing her away from the body. She complies, head down, aware that she has displeased her master.

Des takes the tie from the youth's neck and then sits down and looks at him. For a long time, he does not move again. Even if someone had come in, he would not have flinched for a single moment. He is contemplating this body, staring at it, until he knows what to do.

Something comes to him, and he goes to run a bath. With it nearly full, he stops the water and grabs a towel. The towel is for covering the window, which does not have curtains. He doesn't want anyone to be able to see.

He kneels down in front of the body and gently pulls it forward, over his right shoulder, until he is able to lift it. He grasps the thighs of the body to hold it in place, and carries it into the bathroom. He slides it carefully into the water and washes it all over, with washing up liquid, as if completing a secret ritual. The body is limp and floppy, and moves strangely, making it hard to keep it steady.

When it is clean, he picks up the slippery body again, pulling him by the wrists after other techniques fail. He sits it on the seat of the lavatory and wipes it dry with a towel. Now it is perfect.

Des carries the body over his shoulder, back into the main room, and lays it on the bed.

He tidies himself up, smoothing away the evidence of their struggle and of the messy bath, and then takes a closer look.

The body has a slightly pinkish tinge to the face, the features are a little puffed up, and the lips are blue. The eyes and mouth are both partly open. Running his fingers over it, Des discovers that the body is still warm to the touch, as if alive. There is a wet mark on the pillow from the water left in the hair. Des pulls the covers up to his chin as if to tuck him in for the night, and sits down to stare at him again.

He is waiting for the knock on the door, for the police to come. He sits and stares at the body, so that at least he will have a lasting memory to hold on to when they come and take him to prison.

Chapter Three

Just as he thought, no one notices or cares about what goes on inside the little world of his flat. No one cares about what he did for the New Year. No one will ask, and want to hear the answer.

No one bats an eyelid when he buys an iron pot and an electric knife the next morning, but then, everyone would assume it would be for a family meal. That's what everyone else is using things like that for at this time of year.

He gets home and wants to laugh at himself; he already knows that the idea was a stupid one. He stows the new cooking tools away and forgets about them. There must be another way to deal with the body.

Besides, it is still beautiful and pure. It shouldn't be ruined yet.

Des is exhausted, his head aching; the hangover of all hangovers. He's used to hangovers, granted, but this is a big one. He remembers that he has some new underwear in the wardrobe, still clean and fresh in the packaging: briefs, a vest, and socks, probably a fair fit for the body.

He dresses the youth in these clothes, as if it would be rude to leave it exposed and naked, then takes a bath. He must clean himself from the outside before he makes contact with it again.

The dead youth is starting to feel cold when he gets into bed next to it, but he doesn't mind; not at first. He caresses and soothes it, feeling the smooth skin, slipping his hand into the underwear in a way that seems somehow more alluring than it did before he was dressed. The whole prospect is exciting.

The foreplay is wonderful, but the building tension has to go somewhere. All the touching and caressing leads to an obvious conclusion. Des turns the body over and tries to enter it, but the touch of cold, stiff flesh begins to drain away his enthusiasm. This is only a dead body, this, not the warm and tender boy he saw a day before. Not the kind of body you want to feel yourself inside of. He feels the heat drain away from his own body at the point of contact and gets off the bed.

No one can say he didn't try, but he just couldn't put his heart into it. Not that.

There is no longer any reason to keep the body in the bed, and besides, it is cold. It is not a pleasant bedfellow. Des lays it on the floor and drapes an old curtain over it, then gets into bed and falls asleep.

That evening, Des sits watching television with Bleep padding around the room, and eats dinner. The body lays on the floor in the shroud behind him. Des is starting to mind less and less.

He decides that the right place for this body is under the floorboards. In fact, it makes a lot of sense. Add in some bricks from the garden, a bit of earth to pack the place more tightly, and it's like a ready-made burial ground. Not quite a proper one, but the best he can do in these circumstances.

When he has watched his fill, Des gets up and pries up some of the floorboards, just enough room to push the body inside. He pulls it over, but it is already starting to go stiff. Rigor mortis. The very thing that had caused him to lose his own stiffness; what irony. He cannot get it under the floorboards in this state, so he stands it up and leans it against the wall. How odd, to think of a dead man standing up.

Well, he has heard that rigor mortis passes after a while. That's how the police can tell how long someone has been dead for. He figures he will wait and see what happens, and put it under the floor when it has loosened up.

In the morning, the youth is still propped up against the wall. Des lays him down on the floor and finds that he can work his limbs loose if he carefully massages and moves them around. So, it was true.

This is good news: the body can go under the floor, after all. Before that, Des decides to say a little farewell. He examines every inch of the body: underneath its fingernails even, and between his toes, and between the roots of his hair. He memorises and exhilarates in every part of it.

Just as he is ready to finish the task, the cat appears as if deliberately to make a nuisance of itself. It jumps down into the hole and scampers around, apparently loving the idea of a dark space under the floorboards where it might catch mice or spiders. It runs around for a full ten minutes before Des finally manages to coax it out. Low threats, gentle pleas, proffers of food and treats, all of them seem nothing more than air to Deedee. She is simply done looking around when she comes out. Not like Bleep. Bleep does what she is told.

Finally, Des gets the body under the floor and covers it up, and puts the boards back into place. Then he shreds up all of the clothes the youth was wearing and puts them out in a bin bag with the rubbish. Well. That's an end to that.

A week later, Des sits in the evening and wonders about decomposition. How long does it take for someone to rot, he wonders? He begins to get a little anxious, thinking of the perfectly smooth body that he left under there. Is it rotting now? Is it falling apart?

He pries up the floorboards again, suddenly desperate to check. He has no idea or intention of what to do if it is ruined.

When he pulls him out, he can barely see a thing. All of the earth down there has stained it horribly, covering its flesh and sticking to it. Des strips off so as not to ruin his own clothes, and then takes the dead youth for its second post-mortem bath. Afterwards he has to wash himself off, too: the soil is everywhere.

He lays the body down on the carpet and admires it. It is not discoloured, not rotten, not changed in any way. It is a little more tactile; its limbs move more freely now. It is still perfect.

"Look at you," he murmurs, as if anyone can still hear him.

Des can't stop looking at it – can't stop admiring it. The prone youth. The perfect incarnation of his mirror fantasy, brought here into flesh. Just as the mirror always did, the sight of this body arouses him beyond compare.

He kneels over the body, drinking in the sight and the sensation as he uses his own hands for pleasure, and finishes onto its stomach.

He is ready for bed, now, but has an idea before he gets under the covers. The platform is high enough that the youth could touch it with the tips of his fingers if he stood on the floor. Just the right height. He strings the body up by the ankles, attaching it in such a position that the fingers are just brushing the carpet. A very pretty sight indeed.

He leaves it there all night, hanging, waiting for his pleasure. He sleeps a deep sleep, untroubled and easy, after the satisfaction of the day.

In the morning he brings it down and takes his pleasure again, before wiping the stomach clean with a towel.

Now, to business. He needs to cut it up so that it is easier to dispose of. But looking at it, it's so perfect. So beautiful and pure. No; he can't spoil this marvellous body.

He puts it back under the floorboards.

Chapter Four

He dreams of Aden, of military service, a time when things were so much simpler somehow. He was a young man still, smooth and strong.

He had been down at the bar with some others from the unit, and the drink rushed through his system until he felt as at home as if he were in his own country, not in the middle of a war zone. He forgot somehow that he was an army man in enemy territory, and simply hailed a cab.

It was a big mistake. He remembers passing out on a leatherette seat, unable to stop the world from rolling around him with the motion of the car.

He only wakes up to feel a violent and shocking blow to the back of his neck, knocking him back into oblivion again. He had not even been aware that there was anyone behind him.

He wakes up again a while later, disoriented, pained, still drunk. Sober enough to know that something serious is happening. He is no longer on the back seat of the car, but in the boot. He knows that from the shape of the space around him, the feel of the dark material against his skin.

His naked skin. His clothes are in a pile beside him. Someone has stripped him off, and he feels cool metal against his body too, and cold night air seeping in from somewhere. It is totally dark.

Then he hears a lock turning in front of him; the door of the boot opens upwards and reveals a patch of ground and sky.

He grasps the jack that was laying next to him, the cold metal biting into his hand, and slams it against the head of the ugly, old taxi driver as soon as he can get a good look at him. The old man slumps to the ground, unconscious. He probably used the same weapon to knock Des out earlier.

He grabs his own clothes and dresses hurriedly, then hesitates. The man is still out cold. A last act of revenge, he strips him quickly and unceremoniously. When he runs, he takes the man's clothes with him. The tables turned.

Chapter Five

There are a few rare nights when he manages to hold the attention of a few men at once. Those sometimes feel like the best: holding court, having them all listen to him at once, being the hero who has a flat nearby they can use to carry on drinking in.

This time they walk from the Kilburn High Road and make it back for a few more drinks in armchairs, scattered around the front room like a resting clan. It warms him to have so many guests at once. It feels like things might look up, like he might not have to be alone all of the time.

Ribald jokes, choruses of popular songs, and laughter fill the night. He holds court, leading them all in the evening's entertainment. Though he can't help but let a few political statements slip in here and there, for the most part they are unremarked upon. Tonight, the atmosphere is fun, and relaxed, and isolated from the cold truths of the rest of the world.

It is settled that they will all stay the night, draped over armchairs and beds and floors like so many empty beer cans. Des thinks awhile about how he can impress them; how he can make them want to come again.

He will play the hero, he decides. He likes the fact that they were all so happy to have a place to come back to. Perhaps they will be even happier if he gives them a greater gift than that.

When he is sure that they are all asleep, Des creeps around the house, quietly shutting all of the windows. He takes a jacket and sprinkles water over it, then places it over the stove. This done, and with everything in place, he lights the stove. Immediately, the room begins to fill with smoke.

That is enough for him; he doesn't need to stay and watch it any longer. He grabs Bleep on the way past and goes out into the garden, shutting the door behind him.

Though she may not know what is happening, Bleep is happy for a night time stroll around the garden. She doesn't often get to go out like this. Des is worried that her lungs are too small to inhale the same amount of smoke as a human can without damage, and besides, there is another concern: she's a watchful dog. She tends to bark if she senses smoke, or sees a cigarette dropped onto the floor. A few times, she has probably even saved him from a burned-out flat when he was catatonic from the drink.

He pays close attention, even while he intends his walk to seem casual; if he is seen, he wants to be seen as a man letting his dog out to use the toilet in the night, that's all. At last, he sees one of the men stirring through the window.

That is his cue. What use heroics if there is no one awake to witness them? He rushes back into the house and flings all of the windows open, ripping the jacket off the stove and hiding the evidence as he does so.

Coughing and choking, they get up one by one, rushing outside to breath in the purer air of the cool night.

He has saved them all from certain death! What a gallant figure! What a dashing rescue! And yet, oddly enough, none of them so much as thanks him. They cough and splutter, and he will give them that; perhaps they are in too much shock for the moment to gather their wits and their politeness. Surely, though, they will express their gratitude in the days to come.

But no one calls to arrange a meeting the next week, or the week after that. No one even calls to say thank you. He never hears from a single one of them again.

He is sure that it has worked before. He has done it before, if in a bit of an amateurish way, since it was his first try. He saved a good friend of his, Martin, from smoke once, and the two of them still talk. Maybe he has chosen the wrong people. Maybe he just didn't go far enough.

The only way to be sure is to try it again.

Chapter Six

Martin Hunter-Craig, the friend he used the smoke trick on once before, comes to stay for a few days. Des has always been mildly surprised when he shows up at the door; the man is an anomaly, a returnee who likes to stay in the flat for a few days from time to time. Unlike the others who promise to return but never do, Martin can be counted on to appear from time to time. When he isn't working and he needs a place to stay, he comes to call.

They have a bit of an agreement, a running one which was made the first time Martin visited. That night, Des invited him into bed, and Martin told him he was out of money. They enjoyed one another's company, and in the morning, Des left a pile of notes discreetly on the coffee table for Martin to pick up. Then he told him to come back whenever he wanted.

In some ways, Des knows that Martin abuses his hospitality a little. There are plenty of men who will come to stay with him overnight for free, and be glad of it. There are others who would even pay for the privilege of sleeping in an armchair if it got them off the streets.

But, they get on well, and that is enough for Des. It's good to have someone around who will argue back from time to time. Twinkle never did that; most visitors are too busy trying to play nice to disagree with him. Martin is happy to tell it like it is.

Martin turns up at the door this time with a duffle bag on his back, his long, curly hair ruffled by the wind and a wild look in his eyes as usual. "I was hoping you could put me up for a few days," he says, and Des smiles and steps aside to let him in.

"Waiting on the DHSS again?" Des cracks, closing the door behind them.

"Always," Martin says, turning around and flashing him a wry grin. "Can't book in anywhere until I get the Social Security cheque through. Same old story."

"You'd think they'd sort the system out," Des grunts, sitting down in an armchair as Martin joins him. "Not that it will happen now we've a Tory government again. Those bastards are more likely to snatch the cheque out of your hand altogether."

The two of them slip into easy conversation as if it was only yesterday that Martin was around. In reality, it has been months.

While they talk, Des gets a quiet thrill out of the fact that Martin has no idea there is a body underneath their feet.

In the night, even though Des is barely sober enough to get his words in the right order, he undresses and starts to caress Martin. Martin, as always, is quick to reciprocate. Des sometimes wonders if he is aroused by the thought of being intimate with him, or the thought of the money that will be waiting in the morning. In the short run, at least, it does not matter.

Des lays on his back and allows Martin to take the lead; it's easier that way, the room spinning less. He can barely find the space in his consciousness to instruct himself to move, so he lays stiff and heavy.

"Well, this isn't much fun, is it?" Martin pants out, pausing in his own movements for a moment. "Are you going to move your legs a little bit?"

Des moves a tiny fraction, and then stops again; despite Martin's obvious frustration, there is so little space in-between the alcohol and the arousal that he can barely concentrate on anything else at all.

Martin is exasperated, throwing his hands up in the air and remaining still. "It's like having a relationship with a dead body," he says.

Des laughs out loud. If only Martin knew. If only he had any idea about what it was really like to do that, or that Des had even tried it himself. If only he could imagine that there was a dead body just a few feet away from him, lying under the floorboards, naked and smooth. The idea is so hilarious that Des can't help laughing and laughing.

"It's not that funny," Martin mutters. "I wish you'd be a bit more like this when you're screwing."

Although Des makes only the barest effort to comply, and although Martin can obviously see this, they continue. Martin has a wage to earn, after all, and perhaps he is worried that the money won't be on the table if he doesn't help Des get the full enjoyment out of it.

Still. There's no other rent boy you could imagine in the city of London who would complain that you weren't putting your back into it. That's just one of the reasons why Des doesn't mind having him around.

In the morning, Des cooks breakfast for them both.

"How long are you staying, this time?" Des asks, putting a plate of eggs down.

"A couple of days," Martin says, shrugging. "I should be able to get the cheque tomorrow."

Des sits down with his own food and eyes him carefully. "Look," he says. "If you want to, you can always move in here. It'll save you a great deal of money."

Martin chews a piece of egg thoughtfully, a studied frown appearing between his eyebrows. He nods his head from side to side as if considering it, then swallows the egg with a shrug. "I don't know," he says. "My work, you know. I have to be able to move around. I never know where I'll be next week."

That stings a little. Martin has been careful, diplomatic even, but Des can see the real answer in his eyes. As soon as he heard the question, before he had time to think of something to say, Des could see the spark of discomfort. Martin doesn't want to live with him, and not because he has to move often.

Des won't ask again. Even though he would desperately enjoy the pleasure of having someone around for company, every day – even though he would never ask Martin to join him in the night again – he knows he won't like the answer. They are set in their places now, the host and visitor, and there is never likely to be a way to prise them out again.

The next day, Martin leaves, with no indication of when he might be back.

Chapter Seven

On the 11th of August 1979, the body has been under the floorboards for seven and a half months. It smells, and Des has to keep using mothballs and air fresheners and everything else he can think of, but nothing helps. His perfect body is gone, and in its place is a stinking inconvenience.

Since no one cares about what he does, he builds a bonfire in the garden and places the body in the middle. Then he burns it. Just like that.

The smell is awful, and the only way to bear it is to get so drunk that he no longer worries about whether he is being discreet – and that is a worry in itself. Still, he wraps it in the curtain and gets it out to the bonfire looking like just a pile of rags. When it is in the centre of the flames, it disappears easily enough, and the evidence against him goes with it.

After it burns out, he pounds the ashes until they turn into a fine powder that contains not one scrap of bone material or identifying feature, and then rakes them into the ground. The whole sorry story with the Irish boy is over, and after all, Des has been off the drink and behaving well. There's no need to worry about it any longer, or think about handing himself in to the police. It's over, now. He won't do it again.

Chapter Eight

Two months later, Des is starting to feel normal again. As if he is just the same as the people walking around the streets every day – or at least, the same as the men in the bars he frequents.

He leans against the bar and looks around, and is fairly pleased when a young Chinese man pitches up next to him. He has always liked the look of an Asian man. Small, neat, and exotic. Just his type.

"Hi there," Des says, lifting his pint in greeting.

"Hi," the Chinese man grins. "I'm Andrew."

"Great English," he says. "I'm Des. What brings you to London, hm?"

"I'm a student," Andrew says with obvious pride. "This is a great city for learning."

Des nods. "Aye, it is that," he says, as if he knows. "And the pursuit of learning is a great and valued one. It's a good choice you've made there, hm?"

"Thanks," Andrew says. "What do you do?"

"Oh, I'm in the civil service," Des says, tipping his pint glass in mock salute. "Serving the country, as it were. I'm at the Jobcentre. If you're looking for some part-time or temp work while you study, I'm your man."

"I'm sure you are," Andrew says, his smile and his eyes lingering on Des for just long enough to make it abundantly clear that he is flirting.

Des almost loses his bottle at that. Strange, but until he has enough drink inside him, the nerves tend to take over. He takes a big, long swallow from his pint glass, draining a good amount to bolster himself. That should do the job.

They talk a little while at the bar before the obvious overtures are made, and when Des leaves the pub, Andrew walks with him. They sit in the living room, Bleep banished outside, with glasses in their hands, and Andrew barely bothers to hide his intentions. It all comes to a head when he makes the leap to discussing things openly.

"Have you ever been tied up?" he asks excitedly.

Des gives him a sideways look. "I never have," he says, feeling a sense of annoyance wash over him at the mere suggestion. It's not his kind of play. In fact, it sounds like someone else entirely.

"I have," Andrew proclaims. "It's really erotic, you know? The lack of power."

Des sips at his drink.

"I'd like to tie you up," Andrew says, but then rushes on. "Or you could tie me up, if that's what you prefer."

Des shrugs. "I'm not the tied-up type," he says, hoping that will be an end to it. Andrew knows nothing about power, and being powerless. Not if he hasn't experienced what Des has.

Andrew turns his glasses around in his hands a few times, looking down into the liquid. "It's hard, getting by as a student in London," he says, in what seems like an abrupt change of topic. "I'm always short on money."

Ah. Not a change of topic at all, then. Des sighs, scratches the back of his head. Well, he doesn't want to be alone tonight, after all. "I can give you some money," he says.

"Sure," Andrew says, almost springing forward, an eager look in his eyes. "What do you want to do? I can be a bottom, or-"

Des shakes his head, no. "I'm not interested in that tonight," he says. The truth is, he hasn't attempted anything like that since the failure with the dead youth. He puts the thought out of his head again quickly. The less he thinks about it, the less he engages in that kind of activity, the safer everyone is.

Andrew looks a little crestfallen. "It's just, I really do need the money," he presses.

"It's fine," Des sighs. "I'll pay you. Just for company, mind. I'm not interested in fucking you."

"What am I here for, then?" Andrew asks. He is starting to become angry, the tension bubbling under the surface of his drink and spilling out. Maybe it isn't just about the money after all. Maybe a little wounded vanity. "You're the one that brought me back."

Des taps his glass for a moment, thinking. There's not much in him but anger too, now, and this kid is annoying him far too much. Bringing out thoughts that he doesn't need. What's this all about, anyway? An attempt to rob him, most likely, just like the one who forced the meter when Twinkle was still around. He's not having that happen again.

"Fine," Des announces crisply, getting up all of a sudden and clattering his glass down onto the coffee table. "I'll get some rope."

Andrew is almost giddy as Des ties his feet together, immobilising him. Des hopes that at least it will keep him quiet.

"You're living a dangerous life, you know," he comments, picking up a tie from the back of a chair.

Andrew squirms to look at him, but Des stays behind his back. "I know what I'm doing," he retorts.

"Really?" Des asks. "There are a lot of bad things that could happen to you, trying to mess with people like this, trying to get money out of them."

He slips the tie over Andrew's neck suddenly, feeling a dangerous sensation flash up within him. It's not like with the Irish boy. This time he is only half there, annoyed but not desperate. He pulls the tie tightly, cutting off Andrew's breath, but only for a moment.

"This is the sort of thing that could happen to you," he announces, then releases his grip. Andrew is panicking, flailing around at his neck, trying to get away. Des has no desire to keep this annoying student close; he lets go of the tie entirely.

Andrew starts to move, but his feet are still tied; obviously fearing another attack, and gibbering all kinds of nonsense at him, he grabs up a candlestick and throws it at Des. Des ducks, but the aim was off anyway.

By the time he stands up and looks again, Andrew is just ripping off the last of the rope and scrambling to his feet.

He runs out of the door, and when Des follows him to stand in the entranceway, Andrew is already halfway down the road.

Des stares after the retreating figure, glancing back over its shoulder every few steps with a frenzied terror. He almost wants to laugh. What a situation. That guy talked about getting tied up, but he couldn't handle something so simple as a quick tug on his neck. People can be so full of themselves.

Half an hour later, there is a knock at the door. Des puts his glass down again – it was empty anyway – and answers it, feeling completely unsurprised to see a couple of policemen standing on his step.

"Hello, sir," one of them says. "We've had a report of an attack at this address."

Des lets them in, plays the part: simply a kinky gay sex thing, officer, simply a lover's tiff, a bit of a misunderstanding on limits. He asked to be tied up, officer, he wanted it. I never tried to strangle him, no, he just panicked when I put the tie around his neck.

Des knows what they want to hear. He was a bobby himself a while back; he's been through all the training and he's heard the sordid locker room jokes. All he has to do is play to stereotype and maybe ask after an officer or two to let them know he's one of them.

Later, he hears that Andrew has dropped the charges. It doesn't really surprise him. But in his head, he can't help but keep replaying that moment. The tie in his hands, the strain around Andrew's neck. The panic of the man and his body, restrained, flailing to get away. The moment of power when he could have pressed it closer, could have made him stay forever.

Next time he finds someone he likes, he wonders. Maybe it will be a different story. But for now, he can ignore it, pretend it was nothing. A lot of guys like trying the asphyxiation thing, a lot of men in London like being tied up. It's all normal when you go to the pubs he goes to. It never has to go any further than that again, not if he keeps it under control.

Chapter Nine

Des is in the pub again. The Princess Louise has a beautiful Victorian interior, but that's not what he is here for. Rather, he is here to find himself a bit of company.

He has been eyeing the young man with the camera. He is slight and has dark hair down to his shoulders, and the camera is placed on the bar in front of him. Des heard him ordering a drink, and his voice was polite and well-mannered – and not from around these parts. There was something to it: a twang. American, maybe, he thinks.

"What brand of camera is that?" he asks, on impulse, leaning towards him to make it clear he is addressing the young man.

He looks up from his pint, seemingly a little surprised, a small flush on his cheeks. But he seems happy for the intrusion, not shy. "Oh, it's a Canon," he says quickly, lifting it up to show it off.

"You a photographer?" Des asks.

"Well, it's a hobby," he says, with the air of someone who is playing himself down. "I just like to record what I see."

Des nods. "Right," he agrees. "You're not from around here, hn?"

The young man flashes him a smile. "Neither are you, from the sounds of things," he says, playfully. Des likes that.

He slides his pint a little closer across the bar and hitches over to the bar stool nearest to the young man. "That's right. Scotland, myself. I'm Des."

"Kenneth. Ken," he replies, correcting himself or perhaps just too polite to introduce himself with a nickname first. "Canada. Well, since I was a teenager, anyway."

"Oh, right," Des nods. "Explains the twang. So where did you originate?"

"Croydon," Ken says, with some obvious pride.

Des grins, gives him a little chuckle. "A more local man than me, then, hn?"

Ken laughs at that. "I guess you're right!" he exclaims.

The two of them are laughing and joking in no time. It's 3pm, that odd lull, that moment in the afternoon when lunch is over but dinner yet to come. That moment when you get a restless feeling, a need to do something, a sleepiness, something you can't put your finger on until you do something about it.

"Would you like to do some sightseeing with that camera of yours?" Des asks, finishing his pint and placing the empty glass down on the bar.

Ken glances at his own glass, empty a while ago. "Sure, why not?" he replies.

"I'll give you the tour," Des says, and Ken grins back.

Des likes him. Ken reminds him a little of an ex. They get on like a house on fire already.

Des takes him on a tour of London, the best he can possibly muster. No hits missed. No punches pulled. They tour Trafalgar Square, Pall Mall, the House of Parliament, and everything else he can think of. Ken snaps away with his camera all the while, winding the film on after each shot, a harsh noise that starts to grate on Des' nerves. The early December air is cold, and he is tired of the feeling.

"How about some music?" Des asks, casually. He feels done with walking around the city he already knows. Time to go home and do something he enjoys, instead.

"What kind of music?" Ken asks eagerly. His long hair is the only concession he makes to his tastes in music, but it's an obvious one to read.

"I've got a lot of records," Des replied. "The Who, Rick Waterman – a lot of music like that. We could go back to my flat and listen to them with a drink or two."

Ken's eyes light up and he nods. "Sure, I'd love to," he agrees.

Des is a good host. He makes sure to serve up a good meal of eggs, ham, and chips (something to soak up all the booze). They head to the offy for beer and rum, and then share the headphones, listening one at a time to all of the records that Ken likes from Des' collection. He even takes a few recommendations of records he isn't familiar with.

Des watches him. Watches him listening to music through his headphones. Des likes that music, and he wants to be listening to it himself. This is his home and his records, after all. Already it has occurred to him that Ken is from Canada; that he is here on a holiday; that one day, very soon, he will go home to a place a very long way away. It begins to seem as though there has been no point in getting to know him at all.

He sits in the corner, still drinking his rum. "Alright?" he asks at length.

Ken nods, his voice a little too loud over the noise in his own ears. "Bloody good! Fantastic!" he replies enthusiastically.

Des stares at him for a moment. He sounds like an idiot. *Bloody good guest this,* he thinks to himself. It is almost 1am, going by the clock. He turns the volume on the television up and tries to watch it, while Ken remains engrossed in the records and his beer. He doesn't even try to engage his host in conversation, or take the hint to turn off the music and watch the television with him. There's no togetherness, anymore.

Finally, it's too much. Des can't have someone in his home, in his own home, ignoring him like this and using him for his hospitality. Can't have someone listening to his music all night long. He stands up and walks behind Ken, who doesn't even turn around. He probably isn't aware that Des has even moved. What a guest.

Des grabs the cord from the headphones and pulls it tightly around Ken's neck.

"Let me listen to the music as well," he snarls, pulling tighter still while pulling Ken across the floor. The oddest thing is how the man doesn't struggle. He just allows himself somehow to be dragged around the room, the cord so tight around his neck that his face turns red. Des holds it for a little bit longer, and then he is gone.

Bleep is barking loudly. Des lets go of the cord and turns to her. "Shut up, Bleep," he snaps. "This is fuck all to do with you."

The dog whines, then lowers her head when he grabs her by the collar and forces her out into the garden. One less thing to worry about. He can't have her running around in here with all of this going on.

He looks over at the body lying on the floor, and then goes first to the coffee table. He drinks his glass of Bacardi and coke, almost straight back. Now, he knows, there is work to be done.

The ritual is imprinted heavily on his brain, even though it was no ritual until the first time he did it, even though this is only the second time. First, he peels off the clothes; gingerly so when approaching the trousers, from which a smell is emanating. It appears that Ken messed himself during his last moments. Des carefully and gently cleans him off with a piece of toilet paper before putting him into the bath to make sure that he is really clean. He towels him off gently and then lifts him back into the bedroom.

He lays Ken down on the bed, and goes back to the headphones. He sits and drinks the rest of the rum while he listens to the record. *Hooked On Classics* by the Royal Philharmonic Orchestra. It's a good record. He just wanted to listen to it for himself.

At last, he turns off the record player and gets into bed next to the body. He kisses it, everything forgiven now, and falls asleep.

In the morning, Ken's body is cold. Shockingly so. Des misses the warmth that had coursed through his veins before; that precious warmth that was only around immediately after the incident. Now Ken is just a body, and that means he belongs to Des. That in itself is a prize, and he does not want to be ungrateful, even if he is a little disappointed that Ken can no longer chat away with him about music and cameras.

Des takes all of Ken's belongings and throws them away, including the rolls of film he had so painstakingly shot the day before. It seems a shame, but Ken isn't going to be able to see them anyway. There's no sense in holding on to them only for sentiment's sake.

It is early in the morning, but there still is not much time before he has to go to work. Des needs to do something quickly, and then deal with it properly later, when he gets back.

Des puts Ken's body into the cupboard so that no one will see it if they enter his flat. That seems good enough; why would anyone investigate further? He gets dressed, feeds Bleep, and then goes to work.

He thinks about the body all day at the Jobcentre. It is comforting to think about that and not about the unemployed masses coming to sit in front of him all day. It is more rewarding to imagine what he will do later than to think about the promotion he so rightfully deserved, and yet was being denied month after month.

At lunch time, he goes out and buys a Polaroid camera so that he won't have to stop off on the way back from work. He feels a little stupid to have thrown the Canon away only to buy a new camera, but he needed something that was his. Something that wouldn't be quite so easy to trace back to a missing boy.

He makes plans all afternoon, reading the box that the camera came in and going over the instructions, and thinking about the pictures that he will take.

Finally, the day ends and he can go home to visit Ken. His new doll.

Des wastes no time in getting him out of the cupboard as soon as he is home. To his dismay, a brownish liquid has seeped out of Ken's nose during the day. It has dripped down over his chest and arms, making a terrible mess. Des carefully cleans it off with wet tissue paper so that Ken is as good as new.

He dresses him tenderly in a fresh set of briefs, socks, and vest, all brand new for the occasion. His face is a little red and puffy, so he puts body colour on it to tone him down a little. How funny: once he used it to make himself look dead. Now it is make-up for the dead instead. He lays Ken down on the bed and arranges his body so that he can see him perfectly.

There are 15 shots in the Polaroid, and he uses them all, capturing the moment for eternity.

Then he puts the camera aside, feeling strange things washing over him. At times he can see Ken exactly as he was, a beautiful body, a doll, the perfect substitute for his sexual fantasies. Glorious. At other times he sees the young man who was excited to listen to *Tommy*, and he feels something else entirely.

He lays down and pulls Ken on top of him, holding him there, the two of them together. He turns on the television so that they can watch it, and talks to Ken about the shows on the screen. He alternates between pretending that Ken can see it, and crying. Part of him feels a little unhinged. For the most part, however, he is too wrapped up in Ken to even think about it.

Finally, before going to sleep, he undresses Ken completely and pleasures himself between the body's bare thighs. It is close enough to the real thing. It is enough.

Chapter Ten

He dreams about that first time. That glorious first time with the mirror.

He had never known such a beautiful thing could exist. It was all born out of coincidence: his room in Sharjah was private and had an actual lock, and that was the first thing. The second thing was the mirror they had provided for him, free-standing and full-body, that allowed him to watch himself masturbate in the nude.

There had been a first time watching himself. There had been a first time realising that he could watch the mirror and imagine it to be someone else whilst also being himself: splitting his personality in two, just for that short duration.

Then there was the first time he was a dead man.

The body lying back prone on the bed was a young Nazi soldier. He could not see the youth's face, but he was blond and handsome, and recently killed. His body was lifeless, laying still where it had fallen.

Then the other came along: the old, ugly Arab, the lecherous, disgusting man who wants to have his way with this beautiful fallen soldier. He washes the dead boy's body first, and carries it, taking it to a place where he can do whatever he likes.

Then he has sex with the body. He holds the boy in his arms and screws him standing, the boy's limp body flopping as if in rest. At last, as he comes to his climax, the old Arab loosens his hold and the boy flops openly, still impaled and yet exposed entirely. It is a scene of pure lust. It is a scene of unbridled power of one creature over another.

At first, that fantasy in front of the mirror had frightened him. He had wondered what it meant for him.

Now, he dreams of it again and smiles in his sleep.

Chapter Eleven

In the morning, he smashes the records that Ken listened to. He never wants to hear them again.

He has quite forgotten that he has included some of the *Hooked on Classics* tracks in his tapes until he brings them along for the office Christmas party a little later. Someone else is in charge of playing them, and so he has no warning when one of Ken's songs suddenly starts to play. It gives him a real shock.

His mind starts to race, thinking about the body that he has stashed under his floorboards, the man that he killed only two days ago. He has blood on his hands, fresh blood, and not a single person he knows it.

It shames him that until now, he hardly even remembered that he had done anything at all. The world of work is a separate sphere, a place where he is someone else. Not the same man that did those things.

At moments like this, he can barely believe that he has not been caught. At times, he cannot even believe that he has done it.

The music runs through him like an electric current and changes everything. He had been enjoying the party thoroughly, but once he hears that song he can no longer touch a single drop of drink. He feels nervous, and unsettled. He feels like if he doesn't concentrate hard, everyone will see the truth written bold all over his face.

He goes home, the party ruined. All the way on the journey back, and all the time once he arrives at the flat, he can hear the song in his head. It runs over and over, so strong it seems like a wonder that no one else can hear it. He tries to go to bed, but the song only gets louder and harder to ignore.

"Right," he shouts out loud all of a sudden, knowing that Ken will hear him. "If you want to listen to the music then damn well come out and listen to it!"

He grabs the body out from under the floorboards. There is a carrier bag over the face still, and he leaves it there; he does not want to look at

Ken's face. He pours himself a Bacardi and puts on a tape so that they can both hear the music.

Des stands naked in front of the body, listening to the songs. He trembles from head to foot. He drinks his Bacardi and stands and listens for hours.

When eventually he manages to put Ken away and get to sleep, it is so late that he barely has any time before work. In the end, the only thing to do is to throw himself into the clean-up operation after the party. Ken is there, at Melrose Avenue, waiting for him. The busier he is, the less he has to think about it.

In the days afterwards, he is drawn to the body like a moth to a flame. He cannot leave it alone.

Four times, he brings out Ken's body from under the floorboards, in the special space reserved for it. Four times, they watch television together, and he talks to Ken about what they see. Ken is now a very graceful conversational partner; perhaps better than he was when he was alive. Four times, Des strips his body and wraps him back up in the curtain and puts him under the floorboards.

They no longer have any disputes about the music. Des is very careful about that. He makes sure not to listen to their song again.

"Goodnight, Ken," he says tenderly, as he moves the floorboards back into place.

Chapter Twelve

Des enjoys going to his conferences, as they often turn out to be full of individuals who share his passion for improvement of the workplace. It is disheartening to see how many people simply don't care, and how many others think that the word 'union' is a dirty one. The conferences may not achieve much beyond allowing him to talk to and meet these people, many of whom he actually looks up to, but it is something to do, a trip out of the office.

Talking to others who really believe in the worker, like he does, he can actually imagine that they will be able to do something about the situation. That they will be able to make things better. That confidence tends to disappear soon after he gets home, replaced by a doggedly stubborn refusal to allow the bastards to get him down. He might only be playing the naughty boy at school, disrupting labour supplies and standing on picket lines, but at least he is doing something.

The Southport conference had been fine, but a little disappointing for two reasons: first, he had to leave Bleep with a friend, only to find out that he could have taken her with him after all; second, everyone else seemed to have more time for bed-hopping than for spirited debates. He wonders if he is the only person at the whole conference who didn't sleep with someone.

Now that he is back home, it is time to have a little bit of fun. It feels as if he is owed a little bit of letting his hair down, so to speak.

Des likes going to the stations. Euston is one of his particular favourites. For whatever reason, Euston is where a lot of the runaways end up. They sleep rough or sit out and beg near the entranceways. Some of them just hang around, unsure of what to do or where to go next. A lot of them are happy for anything you can give them, even if it is a bed and a Bacardi for the night.

He is wandering slowly through the area when he hears a hint of a Merseyside accent, and something in him brightens a little. Excellent: a conversation starter. Something he can use.

"I've just been to Southport," he announces, standing near the youth.

The boy looks up at him. "Boss, mate," he says, nodding.

They start to chat a little about the area. What Des saw in Southport, the food, the landmarks.

"I'm Des, by the way," he announces, when he feels he has the measure of the boy. "I live close by here."

The boy looks him up and down quickly, an appraisal that lets him know they are both on the same team. "Martyn," he says, getting up and dusting himself off. "Be good to get a drink and some scran."

They walk together, the agreement made. Although Martyn tries to hold his own in the conversation, Des can see that he is tired. He stumbles his words a little, sometimes. When Des tries to ask anything about him, Martyn is withdrawn. It seems like he doesn't want to talk about his life, why he is in London, or his family. He's probably not supposed to be in London, or in trouble of some kind. Fine enough. Des doesn't mind.

In the back of his head a tiny little voice mentions that it might just be better that way.

When they get back to the flat, Martyn's energy levels do not improve. He manages two cans of beer and looks likely to fall asleep where he sits.

"Why don't you go have a sleep?" Des asks, pointing to the bunk bed.

"Belter," Martyn half-murmurs, hardly able to keep his eyes open anymore. "Thanks, mate. Better than sleeping out there, like."

Des nods encouragingly and helps him to the bed, then leaves him there.

He goes back and sits by himself at the coffee table, switching to a stronger spirit. He drinks a while and ponders things. He thinks about work, though he hardly wants to. He gets so frustrated, thinking about how much more qualified he is than his superiors. How much more passionate and better at his job. They say his union work and his attitude let him down. Let them. Standing up for the voice of the workers is important. The proletariat need looking after. If anything, the conference only reinforced his belief in that.

Time moves at a glacial pace in the dark flat. Martyn is snoring ever so softly. For a long while, or perhaps a short while – he can't tell – Des barely knows what he is thinking about.

All of a sudden, he finds himself climbing onto the top bunk. He has a tie in his hands. He climbs over Martyn, wrapped up nicely in the quilt, and straddles his hips. Martyn's arms are trapped in the quilt and he groggily attempts to move, but he is trapped. The flat is in near darkness; only by the dim side light can Des make out the flash of white as Martyn's eyes open, the first look of fear.

The tie is already around his neck now, and Des pulls it tight. Martyn doesn't have enough room to struggle properly. In many ways it is so much easier than the last times. He just pulls tight until the small, feeble movements stop.

Panting for breath himself, Des realises with a sort of shock that his own bottom is wet. He realises, then, that Martyn has wet himself. The urine has soaked all the way through the bedding and then through his own jeans. What a mess. Well. Time to clear it up.

He gets down from the bunk bed and throws Martyn over one shoulder, bringing him down. To some surprise, he notices that Martyn is still breathing through that contact on his shoulder, the rhythmic pulse of life weak but still there.

Des fills the kitchen sink with water and plunks Martyn's head down into it. With one hand pressing down on his hair, he stays like that for perhaps three or four minutes. There is nothing to count time with, so he simply waits for what feels like the right length of time.

That done, he knows it is over. He carries the body to the bathroom now and strips it, then himself. He has been dirtied by the act this time, and he must wash both of them. He climbs into the bath with the body and washes it at the same time as himself.

When they are clean, getting out proves a challenge. He and the body are both slippery with the water, but he manages to carry it back to bed, leaving the bedding discarded on the floor.

He lays it down, and lays next to it, admiring, touching.

This is the youngest body he has ever seen, he thinks, and the thought is an instant turn-on. It is so smooth and soft, so unburdened by the passage of time. It will stay like this, now.

"Your body will be young forever," he murmurs, kissing it wherever he likes. "You are so young and beautiful."

He holds it close, feeling the way the body fits with his, pressing himself against it. When he has had enough of that he climbs up again, straddling the hips the way he did when he was killing it. He sits there and enjoys himself until the spray of white liquid lands across the body's stomach. For just a moment, he briefly imagines the call of seagulls, far off, and a taste of salt on the breeze.

The moment gone, he wipes the body down and places it into the cupboard, while it is still floppy enough to move around. He knows it won't be long before it is stiff, but in a day or two it will be under the floorboards.

While throwing Martyn's things away, Des notices a left luggage tag for Euston station. He goes to pick it up, partly out of curiosity and partly because he does not want to leave something with Martyn's name on so close to where they met.

There are only a few paltry things inside. A change of clothes or two, some personal photographs, things that no longer mean anything. There is also a set of chef knives, which interests Des greatly. He wonders whether Martyn was a chef, or whether he kept them for protection. At any rate, they are good quality.

He keeps them for a while until they have rusted. He figures this will help to disguise their origin, and finally throws them out.

He does not stop to muse on the fact that the sight of the body did not give him cause for panic any longer, or make him cry in sorrow. It is all just the same as when he was on patrol in Aden and would see the bodies littered there, left on the ground with no thought. A Yemeni body or a body from Merseyside, what difference does it make? A body is a body, and when the body is your own, there is no cause for alarm.

By now, the body he placed under the floorboards last year is smelling badly. Des can't stand the smell anymore, and besides, it is useless to him now. The decomposition has ruined it.

He gets drunk and pours a vodka ready to drink while he does the work; later it will be followed by another, and another, just enough to keep his senses steady and to blot out the worst of it. He is terribly sickened by the sight of blood, and he cannot bear to face it sober. He is anxious even at the mere thought that there will be blood involved.

The dog and the cat are put out into the garden; Des strips himself down; he finds a knife in the kitchen. All his preparations are done, and there is nothing left to procrastinate with. Then there is nothing else for it but to get started.

He brings the bodies out, almost choking on the smell, having to stop to retch as he moves them. Then he uses the knife to cut through rotting flesh and chop solid bone to make them into smaller pieces. There is hardly any blood at all, which pleases him, even if the smells get worse the more he opens up the bodies.

They have to be smaller so that they will fit into the suitcases. A whole man is too big to go in. A whole man fits in the cupboard or under the floor, but not in the old suitcases he had in the cupboard with them.

When they are in pieces, he can finally fit them in. He places the parts inside as best as they will fit and zips them up, out of sight. A pair of legs go here, a couple of hands sandwiched there. An arm and a torso next to them. It feels utterly macabre, but with the lack of blood, it also begins to feel like some kind of odd trick. Like these are not body parts at all. Then his hand will slip and slide on a piece of rotten flesh and he will know that it is real.

He built the garden shed for Bleep, but now it is needed for something else. He puts the suitcases right at the back and spends the rest of the day building a low wall around them. Deodorant sticks, newspapers, old bricks; they all pile in on top.

He does not bother locking the door. No one has enough interest in the garden shed of Des Nilsen to take a look.

Chapter Thirteen

Scene: summer, 1972, Shetland Islands. A busy social club full of officers and privates.

Des knows this scene like the back of his hand, and he doesn't want to relive it. But in the night, with the darkness all around and no one to share his bed, he has no choice.

He is standing at the bar of the club, still a young man himself. He is enjoying a drink and a polite chat with another man. It feels like any normal day. Soon he will know that it is not.

An 18-year-old private walks through the door and an electric shock runs right through Des as their eyes meet. He has fallen in love for the first time, right there and then, even before learning the boy's name.

He can hardly breathe with the shock of the moment, and he fears that it will be written on his face when they first speak. But, somehow, he manages to introduce himself and not make a total mess of the conversation. In fact, they get on well. Des offers to take him under his wing, though perhaps not in so many words, and the private agrees.

From then on, they are inseparable. Des comes up with the welcome excuse of teaching him how to use a video camera and projector so that they can spend more time together, making lots of films about their beautiful posting and the seabirds swooping over the cliffs to the sea. They even film one another, for practice, as Des puts it.

He likes to watch the films back over and over again. He likes to watch the boy; he also likes to watch the moments when the boy was watching him.

What worries him now, these years on, is whether he can really remember the boy's face with total accuracy. Sometimes he thinks that he has been distorting it all these years, making it look more like people he has met since, people he has ended. In his memory, there are hesitant smiles, that he told himself at the time were born of nerves.

Nerves, yes; but not brought on by love. He knows that because they never spoke again after he left the army.

He loves that boy so much that it aches. He remembers the exquisite agony of being without him for even a moment during those months. He remembers how it felt to be left behind, pacing his room and trying to think of an excuse to be with him again. It was torture, but it was bliss. It was beautiful and awful and it was everything.

He replays the one time their hands had clasped, the boy crying with homesickness, Des providing the only refuge in this wind-battered outpost. He remembers the guilty way that the boy pulled away when the tears stopped.

He does not want to remember the night when he told the boy to go into the laundry room with him.

"We can go into the laundry, if you like," he says in a memory that haunts him still. "I've got the only key. We won't be disturbed."

"I don't know what's happening," the boy blurts out, his eyes wide with fear. He pulls away from Des and runs down the corridor. Des knows that he has lost him for good in that moment. He knows that the second he tried to make the dream real, it vanished, like so much smoke running through his fingers.

When it is time for him to leave the army, he burns all of their films. The boy has drifted away from him already, pushing him away like yesterday's news. A bad smell that lingered. He burns them in spite and in pain, and now, years on, part of him wishes he had not.

What he wouldn't give to watch one of those films again, now.

Destroying them did not burn away his misery. He had thought about throwing himself off the cliff and into the sea. What misery might have been avoided for so many other boys if he had ended his days there, the seagulls swooping overhead.

Chapter Fourteen

Martin visits again, and Des is pleased to see him, even if he knows the visit will be fleeting.

They settle down in front of the television together. Des already has his Saturday planned: watch a few films, head out to the pub, come back and finish getting drunk, and then to bed. Throw in a walk for Bleep here and there and the day is all figured out.

He is flicking through the channels to find a film when he sees a Western. He smirks to himself and leaves it on, waiting for Martin's reaction.

"You know I hate Westerns," he says after a moment or two, predictable as always.

"I love them, Skip," he says. "Since we happen to be in my home and not yours, I think that settles it, hn?"

He inwardly congratulates himself on the added insult. Skip, short for Skipper, because whores always hang around the docks.

Martin grumbles something quiet and sits back to watch the film anyway, staring sullenly at his can of beer instead of the screen for the most part. Every moment of it tickles Des' humour. He is in control here. Martin has to watch whatever he is told, or he'll be out on the streets instead.

When the film ends, they gather themselves up and go out to a pub. Des chooses one at random for no good reason, but then insists upon it even when Martin expresses another preference. He likes to be the one making the choice.

The night goes well, except for one man standing at the corner of the bar. Des is sure that he catches the man muttering to his companion about them, pointing at Martin and then at Des. The companion laughs and then glances over at them with a smirk. Des downs the last of his pint and drags Martin out of the pub. He's had enough of that.

On the Tube on the way home, he paces around the small space at the front of the carriage, swaying in time with the train's movements.

"That bastard was laughing at us," he says, clenching and unclenching his fist.

Martin sighs. "Don't fly off the handle about this one, Des," he says.

"Oh, she's going to start this one again, is she?" Des snaps. He knows that Martin hates it when he calls him 'she'. That's why he does it.

"Just don't take it personally," Martin tries. "You don't know what he was saying."

"I saw him pointing," Des says, feeling the rage build up inside of him like a vice around the inside of his throat. "At *you*. And then looking at me. He thinks I'm your client. He knows you're a dirty street whore, right? He was laughing at me for paying you."

"So why didn't you confront him about it?" Martin asks, suddenly leaning forward, getting into Des' face. "Why didn't you put him right?"

Des falters for a moment. He has a burning shame at the back of his mind: the knowledge that he would not have been able to go up against the man in a fight. The knowledge that any time he's met any kind of violence outside of his flat, he has been the loser. "I'm far too intellectual for the likes of him," he says dismissively, screwing his face up in a grimace so that Martin won't see the truth in his eyes. "He wouldn't even be able to understand what I was saying. Dumb pricks like that won't listen, hm? No point in talking to them at all."

"Yeah, of course," Martin bites back. His tone hovers on a knife-edge: just bitter enough that Des can tell he is being sarcastic, but just deferential enough that they can both pretend he is merely agreeing.

Martin was supposed to stay for another day, but he leaves early in the morning. He says he will be back. For a change, Des believes him; he knows that Martin actually likes him, no matter how much they fight. And when he needs a roof over his head and a bit of spare cash, he will be back around like a stray cat, begging for milk.

"I like having you around, Skip," he says wistfully as Martin gathers his bag at the door. "It stops me doing naughty things."

As Martin goes, a bemused expression on his face, Des feels a familiar spectre settling over him again. When Martin is around, he knows he is safe. Now? It is anyone's guess.

Chapter Fifteen

After a while, they all start to blend together. Those that don't leave the pub with him. Those that come back for a drink. Those who he hovers over, thinking, until the urge goes away. Those who never leave the flat again.

He's in a pub near Piccadilly Circus when he meets a fellow Scot. A tall man from Edinburgh, probably in his mid-twenties, already worn a little with life. But the accent sounds like home and he has a wide grin somehow, a kind of easy smile that seems to sit on his face without shifting.

"A countryman," Des says, leaning next to him at the bar.

"Oh, at last, someone sensible in this city," the other man grins, and Des knows that he is as happy to hear a familiar accent as Des is. Sometimes, even when 'home' is the last place that feels like home, you can still miss it when you aren't there.

"I wouldn't know about sensible," he says, laughing and picking up his pint as if by way of illustration.

The other man laughs too, and claps him on the back. "Aye, well, no, you're right there," he concurs, indicating his own drink. "I'm Billy."

"Des," he replies, nodding. "No word of a lie and all joking aside, I'm happy to hear a Scottish voice tonight."

"You can hear a lot more of this one, my man, so long as I can hear one too," Billy proclaims. He has the air of someone who is just a little too weary with life, but still gamely trying to carry on as best as he can, without anyone seeing the cracks underneath the smile. Des can relate to that, at least in part, and they end up sitting together to continue their conversation.

He talks just a little more than Des likes, but at least he talks.

Someone nudges Des in the elbow while his new drinking companion is in the toilet.

"You wanna steer clear of 'im, mate," his fellow customer says in a low drawl. "Seen 'im 'ere a couple o' weeks back. He's one o' them, you know. Wants paying for it."

Des nods at this information, narrowing his eyes a little, processing. "Thanks, mate," he manages, but in the end, he concludes that it doesn't bother him very much. Not if Billy doesn't expect payment on top of the drinks for a bit of talk. When he gets back, Des doesn't mention what he was told. He doesn't want to sour what might be an entertaining evening.

Billy has a mop of dark, curly hair that moves when he laughs and nods his head. They are getting on fine, and Des doesn't mind paying for another drink or two, so he decides it's time to get away from prying eyes.

"Come on," he says. "I know a place much better than this."

Billy follows him eagerly, and somehow that desire to escape escalates into a pub crawl that takes them writhing across the city. Time goes on, however, and Des finds that he might prefer his own company tonight after all. He has that sour taste in his mouth, that world-weariness. He's fed up of walking in the August air, so full of a dark tension yet to be relieved by a storm, and he wants to go home. Tonight, it sounds like sitting in the dark and waiting for sleep with a glass of vodka or so might actually be inviting.

They head for a pub in Charing Cross Road and Des finds that one more drink is quite enough. He looks at Billy's knuckles, tattooed with the ever-obvious 'LOVE' and 'HATE', and knocks back the last of his pint.

"Alright, then," he says, getting up from the bar stool. "I'm off." And he means it.

Des walks down the stairs at Leicester Square and walks over to the ticket queue, waiting his turn. He picks up the familiar ticket and turns to go, reflecting on a night now over.

Billy is standing in his way.

Des fixes him with a look, and Billy manages something close to a blush.

"I, uh," he starts, shrugging his shoulders awkwardly. "I've nowhere else to go."

Des sighs. He knows deep inside that he honestly doesn't want to, but all the same, he buys another ticket for Billy. He hands it over with a reluctance that must show on his face, but Billy doesn't seem to care. He must be desperate.

They sit down in the flat and they listen to music and they drink. It's always the same story. Des looks over at him listening to the music and after a while he goes to sleep.

When he wakes up in the morning, he is almost – but not quite – surprised to find a body in the bed with him. He remembers something about his hands, tightening, pulling something, and he remembers vaguely looking into Billy's face while he does it.

Now, there's just another body, and he feels a little cheap somehow. Like getting too drunk to remember sex. Missing a memory that should be special, but wasn't, because you had ruined it.

He has already undressed the body and washed it. He knows this much because it is wearing a new set of briefs, vest, and socks, taken from his specially prepared stash for just this occasion. He admires it now in the light of day.

Fair enough, this one is a little far from his ideal. The tattoos across the chest and the arms, the hair. He shaves it carefully and it looks a little younger after that. Talcum powder lessens the effect of the tattoos somewhat. He dresses it up, and in the end finds that it fits his fantasy just fine, tattoos or no tattoos. Certainly not a patch on the last one, but it's a good body all the same.

He arranges it carefully in a few different positions, trying to ignore the tattooed areas and focus on the parts that look younger. Smoother. He masturbates onto the body's stomach and cleans it up again. The discovery of a body, almost like a surprise, is a new element to this fantasy made real; it reminds him of opportunistic characters from his mirror stories, coming across a body left in the woods to drag it back home. It's not so bad that the body is here, after all.

But it is still a body, and not one he had planned for. It can only amuse him for so long.

It goes under the floorboards with the rest.

Chapter Sixteen

The fantasy is always growing, always developing. A few short years ago he could never have imagined having these real bodies to play with; creating a new kind of flatmate that would stay with him forever, at least in some form or another.

Back then he had the mirror, and the mirror treated him well. He closes his eyes and remembers the details of those many delicious nights.

In the memory he puts talc onto his face and body, which will remove the impression of living colour and make him pale as death. Charcoal is used under his eyes: he smears it around until he creates a hollow, dark look, helped by his own lack of sleep. He adds pale blue colour to his lips. He rubs his eyes hard until they are bloodshot and red.

In a way, this is like his own kind of drag. He doesn't want to be a woman, not ever. But he can be something else instead.

He has an old t-shirt which he poked three holes in at another time, and the mirror propped up against the bed ready for him. The last touch is a mixture of cochineal and saffron. He puts this together himself so that he can synthesise a kind of blood.

The blood soaks into the holes of his t-shirt, running down in gouts as if rushing out of a fatal wound. It runs down not only the shirt but also his skin, warming on him and becoming more real every moment.

Now he lies in front of the mirror and stares at himself. He allows saliva to foam up in his mouth and drip out, as if he has been shot dead. He stares with fascination at this shot body, bleeding and gone.

Of course, he is not alone. There is always someone else in the room. This time it is an old hermit, who has seen a French student shot dead by the SS in the woods. The hermit lives here in the woods, and he sees everything. He drags the body back to his hut, so he can toy with it.

First, the hermit says, "You have no need for clothes anymore. Let's get them off you."

Then he strips the dead student, and pulls his naked body onto the floor. He gets a cloth and some water.

"They made you terribly dirty," he says, tenderly washing the body, making the blood go away.

The body never replies, but the hermit keeps talking, as if they are having a conversation with two sides.

"We'll make you comfortable yet," he says. "Oh yes. Just a few things to take care of first. You have to be ready, you can't sit around like this all the time."

He ties Des' penis – the body's penis – and puts some wadding in the anus, and then picks him up and puts him over his shoulder. He carries him outside and digs a hole in the woods and buries him there. Not like a grave, not like growing a plant. More like a hidden treasure to come back to later.

The hermit digs him up one day, and brings him back inside, and masturbates over the body. Miraculously, at that moment, the penis comes back to life too, and ejaculates.

Des opens his eyes, and he is in his room, lying on the bed in front of the mirror. Time to tidy up and take Bleep for a walk, he thinks.

Chapter Seventeen

Des is propping up the bar in the Salisbury Arms. He feels a little lonely tonight. There's plenty of time to meet someone, to take them home. He thinks he wants someone to listen to music and drink with tonight.

There is a guy who looks like a good mark. He's slim, young – probably just within his twenties, Des thinks. He looks at him out of the side of his eye, assessing. The guy is on his own, not checking the door or his watch; not expecting anyone, then. Still, he glances around the room occasionally.

Des just about has him pegged as a rent boy, and wonders if he would come back to the flat on the promise of free drinks and food. They won't have sex, so the expense won't be incurred. The guy hasn't picked anyone up yet, so maybe he'll welcome the offer.

Des sidles over, greeting him with a mutter. The guy is foreign, maybe Mexican or Filipino or something like that. Something that gives him bronzed skin and an exotic look. Des decides he looks like a gypsy, even down to his clothes and his hairstyle.

They chat a little while. The gypsy seems open to the offer, and a couple of hours later they find themselves swaying down Melrose Avenue, the cold air snatching away some of their hard-bought numbness.

Some cooked eggs and sausages and beers pass and they end up so drunk they can hardly walk straight, both of them, and both of them somehow end up stripping all their clothes off.

"No sex, right," Des says, reinforcing the notion even as they pull off their underwear.

The gypsy laughs in return as he unveils his body, and they drunkenly make their way up the ladder to the top bunk bed, falling in a heap of sprawling legs and milk-white skin juxtaposed against honey.

Des barely remembers it later, but he climbs on top of the gypsy when some hours have passed. He straddles him, knees on either side, the back of his head pressed against the ceiling. The gypsy half-stirs and seems to view this as a come-on, a late-night change of heart, and doesn't struggle.

Until Des wraps his hands tight around the gypsy's throat and pulls until he doesn't feel any more movement.

I want to see him, he thinks, and half-falls down the ladder in the darkness to fumble his way to the light switch.

He brightens the room, turning on every light and every lamp, which rouses Bleep. She whimpers, raising her head, and Des pats her head and strokes her fur until she goes back to sleep.

Now, back to the business at hand. He gets up again and puts a chair near the ladder so he can stand on it. He pulls all the sheets aside and pulls on the body's ankles until it comes into his arms, then climbs down.

He turns to the mirror. He sees, simply sees, drinking in all that he can. His own naked body, the naked gypsy in his arms, the warm-toned flesh against his own. Himself carrying the prone, dead, helpless body, unveiled and uncovered, completely vulnerable. The head, arms, and legs drooping limply as if he was merely asleep.

Des looks and looks as his arousal grows, until he can no longer stand it. He is sweating with desire, his hearting beating faster than it ever does in his normal life.

He carries the body to the bath and follows his ritual, cleaning and purifying them both, setting the body on a chair and drying it carefully with a towel. The flesh is steaming from the hot water, reacting to the cold air of the flat. Whenever he moves it, a deep sigh comes from the throat, air rushing out as if he were still alive.

He dresses the body in the socks he wore when he came in, but adds his own t-shirt and underpants. He does not bother to dress himself. He wraps the body up in the bedclothes and holds it, then smokes a cigarette.

To complete the picture, he gets up, pours himself a vodka, and puts on a record. *Fanfare for the Common Man* by Aaron Copeland. The sound of discovery, but written originally for war. An inspiration; a farewell.

He gets back into bed and holds the gypsy and cries. He knows what he has done.

It is not just a pretty picture composed for the screen. Even though it sometimes feels as though his whole life is nothing more than a film, Des knows that it is real. This body is real, and the person it used to be was real, and he is no longer real because of what Des has done.

"Don't worry," Des says, holding him tighter. "Everything's fine. It's fine. Sleep."

The music fades out. It is done. There's no use in wasting it now.

Des starts to explore the body, holding it tight with his penis between its thighs. He strips off the underpants and the bedding, and masturbates while holding the body's genitals.

Finally, he cleans it off with a paper towel so they can sleep together, the body locked tight in his arms.

In the morning, he pushes the cold and stiff body away, suddenly repulsed by it. *This is absolutely ridiculous*, he tells himself. He puts the naked body into the cupboard and goes to work.

In the evening when he arrives home, it is like stepping into an alternate world. He gave not a single thought to the body in his cupboard while he was at work. He now gives not a single thought to the person he was all day. He gets changed and eats first, feeding the pets, taking care of the chores.

At last it is time to bring out the gypsy. He cleans it up and dresses it, then sits it down in the armchair so that they can watch TV together. He talks to it, tells it what he thinks about the shows they are watching, and shows it his cleverness through all of the cynical remarks and witticisms he makes. He holds the cold hand.

Bleep somehow ignores the body. It is as if the dog knows that life has fled those fleshy confines and does not bother to come near. Where there is no warmth, the dog knows there is no life or comfort.

Finally he places the body on the table and slowly strips it from top to bottom, examining it closely, from front to back. He thrills and delights in the ownership of this beautiful possession, this thing that he is in total control of. He fondles the buttocks and is still somehow amazed that the body gives no reaction.

Funny, now, how after the body is dead, the penis looks so small and shrivelled. Perhaps it is the first thing to really die.

At least there is one good thing for this gypsy, one silver lining. No one has ever appreciated him like this. He deserves to be appreciated like this, and at last he has it. Des holds him close and poses with him in the mirror.

He wonders if there is some way that he can preserve the genitals. Later, of course, he will dispose of everything – something he does not wish to think about fully just yet – but there are parts he would like to keep. It is a shame that he cannot get his hands on the proper preservative fluids. That would be a wonderful thing, to keep the genitals in a jar and look at them whenever he wants to in the future. Perhaps it's something he can think about later, should any such fluids become available to him.

Perhaps if he does it quickly enough, they won't shrivel at all. That would be a joy to see.

A wonderful week passes in the company of this body. At last, it reaches the point where Des can no longer keep bringing it out of the cupboard. He puts it under the floorboards instead.

Later he considers bringing him out again, but it would not be right. He should be resting under there forever. Des is only forlorn that he cannot provide a bed of white roses for him to spend his eternal rest.

Chapter Eighteen

Is it a dream, or a nightmare? He can hardly tell: the images are grotesque and terrible, and yet he feels an overwhelming sense of love.

He is almost six years old and his mother is telling him to go into the front room of their tiny house. She is telling him that he needs to see Grandad laid out.

He doesn't understand what laid out means, or why he has to see it, but it doesn't particularly matter. He loves his Grandad very much and is always happy to spend some time with him. He rushes through with joy, happy that Grandad is back from his latest trip out to sea.

But his Grandad is acting very strange. He is laying there with his eyes closed in a plain wooden box. He is dressed in white long-johns and he looks like he needs a shave. There is something different about him. Something Dennis can't put his finger on.

No one says a word or tells him what is going on. He peers into the box, unsure about what to think.

"Why does Grandad look so strange?" he pipes up at last, willing to risk a stern look or a word from his mum.

"He's gone to a better place now, lad," Granny says gently, with something heavy in her words that Dennis can't understand any more than he can the content.

He doesn't have any idea about what is going on, and Granny has confused him more than she has helped. What better place is that? Wasn't he right here in their front room? Was he maybe sick, and Dennis would be able to see him again when he was better? Would the wooden box help, somehow?

What did it mean to be in two places at once? To be gone, but here? He begins to realise that Grandad is not waking up or moving, and to see that this is a state that will last for some time; but when will it end?

As he begins to wake from the dream, Des for a very brief moment imagines looking back into the coffin and seeing the gypsy's face instead.

When he surfaces into the waking world, confusion claws at him until he remembers that he is Des now, a man, no longer a shocked little boy with no idea about what he was looking at, or how it would affect the rest of his life.

Chapter Nineteen

At work, Des spots a rare opportunity to actually make a difference. He has been looking for one of these for a long time, and now that it is here, he cannot turn it down.

He gets a request from the police for some emergency catering staff. Fair enough, and he would normally not think twice about it. He has plenty of people waiting to fill exactly these kinds of vacancies.

But it is the address that gives him pause.

He knows that the steel workers' union is currently on strike; coincidentally, the police are asking for catering staff to go to a location near to where they are holding their picket lines.

He double checks the information, and he knows that he hasn't got it wrong. It looks like the police are gearing up to respond to the ongoing dispute.

Des knows what he is supposed to do: gather the workers, send them off to do the jobs, and then turn to the next task. But he also knows what he has to do.

He picks up the phone and checks for the number of the steel workers' union head.

They aren't happy with him for warning the union. He knows that. But he also knows that he himself is a union man, and to do anything else would have gone against everything he signed up for. Besides, how could his own union trust him at all if he was willing to throw another under the bus?

The scrapping of the 1974 Civil Service Pay Agreement is also causing a lot of trouble at work. Des gets his head together with a few others in the office and they talk about what they have to do. They know that they might well be frowned upon for doing anything at all, but at the end of the day, this is their pay that is at stake. Their livelihoods.

Eleven staff walk out with him on the day. It's a rousing success, even if it sounds like a small number.

It's a bit of a coup, too: coincidentally, the day chosen for the strike is the same day that the branch is celebrating its golden 50th anniversary. That gives Des a smirk, really it does. All those government officials and high and mighty somebodies visiting their branch, only to be confronted with the reality of the working class in Britain: fed up and off home.

If only more of his colleagues would join them – but they won't, even when tries to remind them that only blockheaded traitors would choose to side against their own fellow working man. Some people just can't be shown the right path.

Chapter Twenty

He is in a West End pub the next time he meets a likely fellow; someone who will come back to the flat with him, perhaps. When the pub closes, Douglas does indeed agree to go back for a late-night drink, and although he is not gay, Des is at least glad of the company. Why not? An empty one-night stand is no better than an empty one-night friendship; at least in the case of the second, there may actually be some chance of the relationship continuing.

He is just so sick of the pub scene, the way that everything is so temporary. If anyone ever cared to stay more than a night, perhaps he wouldn't need to do the things that he has done. If he could keep the loneliness at bay with a real partner of his own, things would be different. But that's the pub scene. Always transitory.

They drink and listen to music until 1am, so there is not much talk. At least he is not alone, Des thinks.

"I ought to make my way home," Douglas says suddenly at around 1 in the morning, which Des dismisses as ridiculous immediately.

"It's far too late," he says. "You're welcome to stay here. I'm off to bed. You're welcome to join me, if you like."

Douglas visibly balks at the idea. "No, thanks," he says. "I don't do that sort of thing. But I wouldn't mind sleeping here in this armchair."

Des nods, and leaves him to it. There's no reason to argue. He knew already that Douglas wasn't going to be sharing the bed for anything but warmth.

Still, it all irks him a little. Something about the situation, whatever it is, calls to that thing inside of him. Maybe it is the fact that he has not received the companionship he wants. Maybe it is the look Douglas gave him when he suggested sharing the bed. Either way, he gets up after Douglas is asleep and retrieves some string from the kitchen.

He manages to tie Douglas' feet together before he even wakes up. The man must have been tired.

He walks around behind him, slips the tie around his neck, and begins to pull on it. Now, Douglas wakes. Now, Douglas fights like a wild thing, arms waving behind him madly. He scratches Des and the pain jolts something inside of him.

Des falls to the ground as they fight and lets go of the tie. He touches a finger to the scratch and sees blood on his finger. Somehow, it means nothing to him.

"Take my money and go," Des shouts, his voice loud and clear. Loud enough to be heard outside of the flat. He wants something to build on if he needs it later, something that will turn the police away. The shout stops Douglas in his tracks for a moment, as if he realises the intention behind it immediately.

"I didn't come here to rob you," Douglas says, coughing and rubbing his throat, drinking in air as if it is some kind of elixir.

There is a strange atmosphere between them, now. It is as if Douglas does not know what to do. The others have found it simple: either they knew what Des was doing and they ran, or they had no idea and they simply left at the appointed time. Douglas knows, but now Des is not chasing him or fighting him. Des is simply sitting on the floor. What is he supposed to do with that?

"I could kill you right now," Des says calmly, his voice somehow hollow. He does not feel concerned about the fact that Douglas is stronger, ready to fight, and has already beaten him once.

Des has a large bread knife in his right hand; he had brought it in earlier, and he reached for it as he fell. Now he sits and stares at it. He feels stuck between two places. To make Douglas stay forever, or to let him go. Which of the two options, he wonders, would be most likely to put him in jail?

"I enjoyed the music, earlier," Douglas says, out of the blue. His tone is calm, even if falsely so, and Des finds a measure of comfort in it.

"I find music one of the most pleasurable ways to pass the time," Des says, nodding.

"You've got good taste," Douglas says, his voice more relaxed even though he stays standing. He looks as if he might run out of the door at any minute.

"Thank you, I pride myself on that," Des says. He feels gratified. "I am often asked to put together mixes for office parties and the like."

"I can see why," Douglas replies. There is a hint of a smile in his voice, though Des can't look away from the knife for long enough to check whether there is one on his face, too.

"I spend a lot of time listening to music, here," Des admits. "Especially when there is no one else to listen to it with."

Douglas sighs. "Well, it's hard being single in a big city," he says.

"The loneliness is the hardest thing to bear, eh?" Des agrees. He is beginning to feel pacified. It is almost as if Douglas understands.

"It's like a weight," Douglas says, and this hits home like an arrow.

Des feels able to look around now, though he still holds the knife. "Not many people understand that," he says.

"I don't know," Douglas replies, quietly. "I think more people do than let on. Most people are terrified of it."

"Aye, and some don't have a choice but to bear it," Des shoots back. He is his old self again, enjoying the back-and-forth.

Douglas, though, is beginning to seem a little uncomfortable with the subject matter. "The West End, though. Full of great pubs," he comments.

"I like a lot of them," Des agrees amiably. "I mean, it's hard to choose a favourite, really. So many different options, each of them ripe for the right kind of night."

"That's right, you can drink in a different one every time if you want to," Douglas nods. "You don't even need to have a favourite."

"I like to mix it up," Des says. "Some places you can count on being a bit more rowdy. Some pubs are for a certain kind of clientele. Some are quieter, some friendlier."

"We're pretty lucky, having all this choice on hand," Douglas smiles. This time, Des sees it.

"You can say that again," he agrees. "Back home, where I grew up, there was not much choice at all. Not much to do of any kind, truth be told."

Casually, almost without thinking about it, he puts the knife down on the floor.

"Back home," Douglas says, and blows out some air from his cheeks. "Actually, it's pretty late, isn't it?"

"Very late," Des agrees. He gets up, dusting his knees off with his hands.

"I'd better walk back," Douglas says quickly, already moving towards the door. "I had a bit of a sleep so I'm fresh. I'll see you again sometime."

"Right," Des answers, feeling a little lost. There is nothing he can do to intervene; Douglas is already at the door and shows no signs of slowing down. Before he can voice any other kind of farewell, the other man is gone.

Des sighs, and looks around at the room. He tidies up a little, then wanders back through to the bedroom. A bit of sleep is probably what he needs, too.

There is a sharp rap at the door which jerks him awake before he has even properly got his head down. Muttering under his breath, he walks to the door and opens it, wondering if it is Douglas here to pick up something he left behind.

It is Douglas; but not how he expected, and not alone.

Two police officers stand in the doorway, Douglas framed between them a little distance behind, as if reluctant to come forward.

"Oh," Des says, surprised. "Hello. Can I help?"

"We've had a report of a disturbance on the premises, sir," one of the policemen says. "Would you mind if we had a word?"

"Disturbance?" Des repeats incredulously.

He lets the policemen in, and they talk while Douglas hovers nervously outside.

"We've had a complaint from this gentleman that you attacked him," one of the officers says.

"Is that what he called it?" Des asks. Though he can barely believe he is doing it, he drops a little inflection into his words, a little flounce. There's such a thing as a gay stereotype, and even though it might not be helping to alleviate misconceptions, playing to it might just help his case.

"Is your side of the story different, Mr Nilsen?" the officer asks.

"I'll say," Des replied. "He's the one that wanted to get all tied up and play-act. It's not my thing, you know. When I told him I wasn't really interested, he flipped a gasket."

"So you're saying this was a disagreement about your..." the officer hesitates, his lips curling back as if he can hardly bear to say the words. "Sexual relationship?"

"We only met tonight, in the pub," Des says. "I wouldn't say relationship. But yes. He was very insulted when I said I no longer wanted any of it. I asked him to leave because it's my house, you see. Actually, I was thinking about calling you myself."

"Oh?" the officer remarks, looking up with an eyebrow raised, a pencil hovering just above the surface of his police notebook.

"I think it was all a scam to rob me, personally," Des says. He leans forward with a conspiratorial air. "Actually, I wouldn't be surprised if he comes to me in the morning and offers to drop the charges in exchange for a bit of payment. It's all completely ridiculous. I mean, I live a quiet life out here, nothing out of the ordinary like that."

Eventually, he tells enough lies that he thinks they might even believe him.

"We'll be in touch if we need to follow anything up," one of them says, putting his hat back on. "In the meantime, we're treating this as a domestic disturbance with no need to follow through on the charges. Just try to make sure that you know your sexual partners a little better before inviting them home in the future, Mr Nilsen."

Des nods vapidly, as if what the policeman said makes total sense. "Of course, officer, I apologise for all the fuss," he says, watching them leave.

He stands at the door and sees Douglas off, flanked by the two officers like bodyguards. He can't hear them talking up the road, but he can see how Douglas reacts. Angry; disbelieving. He is pointing at the red mark on his neck, but the police officers are shaking their heads.

Des heads back inside, and goes to sleep.

Chapter Twenty-One

It is late 1980 and five bodies have gone under the floorboard in the flat where Des sleeps. This urge he does not understand. There seems to be no difference between the nights that end well and those that don't. The main difficulty lies in deciphering which is which.

It is closing time in the pub and Des wants nothing more than another pint. Just one more to drown it all out. But he and the other drinkers are unceremoniously turfed out onto Charing Cross Road when the time comes.

Amongst them is a man who seems out of place more than the rest. Thin to the point of emaciation, his cheekbones sticking out under a mess of hair, though he must be in his twenties.

Des wonders what kind of awful life might have led him to this point at such an early age.

When they get to talking, the man shows a mouth partly empty of teeth. It is obvious from the trench coat and outsized trousers he wears that he is a vagrant; they do not talk about it. It is so obvious that it almost seems it would be rude to mention it. Like telling a man with a port wine stain that he has a red face.

The pale vagrant comes home with Des, probably excited at the prospect of a night under a roof with a bed to lay on. The news of food and drink is music to his ears too. He needs it, that much is clear.

When he strangles him with the tie, Des feels like he is on some kind of strange high, exhilarated with the goodness of his deed. He is like a god, liberating this poor vagrant from the long suffering that his life has been.

The vagrant's legs rise in the air as he dies, his lungs burning for breath. It looks as though he is trying to ride an invisible bicycle. He is so thin and weak that it is the easiest Des has ever known; like taking candy from a baby.

When it is done, Des almost expects the man to turn and thank him. He would no doubt think it a great favour.

There is no room for another under the floorboards. Besides that, the smell problem is starting to get worse again. He dismembers one and leaves it wrapped up under there to take up less room, and the vagrant goes in. But still, there's that problem of the smell.

The bodies are so dull to him now. Relics of moods which have now passed. He steels himself for the part he dislikes the most and cuts the rest of them up. They fill all of his suitcases completely; the arms and hands of the vagrant do not even fit.

At first, he is not sure what to do with them, but then he remembers the bush outside the French windows. It is a good hiding spot, so he digs a whole there and leaves the hands and arms inside, out of sight. At least that takes care of those.

There is surprisingly little blood when he cuts up the bodies, but he still takes care with them. Each part, after having been removed, is washed and wrapped in paper towels. Then they go into plastic bags, with a separate bag for all of the organs – the parts that smell the worst.

He takes the head first, then the hands and feet. Next, the organs, the arms, and the legs below the knee.

He sweats and swears and drinks. He doesn't care if the neighbours wonder about the noise or what he might be doing.

Next go the chest and the ribcage separately, then the whole area from the buttocks to the thighs. If there are maggots on the body, he uses salt to get rid of them and brushes them off.

Sometimes he is violently sick.

The organs are eaten by wild animals, or perhaps local cats and other pets whose owners do not suspect they have been feasting all night. All he has to do is leave them outside, and they will be gone by the morning.

That just leaves the suitcases full of parts, which have been waiting in the garden shed for far too long.

At last, he cannot wait any longer. Des builds a bonfire on the waste land just beyond his garden. He uses an old poplar tree which had been felled and left to rot; pieces of wooden furniture which he had found abandoned in the neighbourhood; any scraps of wood he can find that will build it taller.

When he is done for the night, the bonfire is five feet tall.

The next morning, he rises early to place his precious bundles inside the centre of the bonfire. It requires a bold heart. He crosses the garden in full sight of neighbouring windows; he takes them through a hole in the fence created by moving the wooden panels; he drags them across the empty land; finally, he pushes and eases them into the bonfire's heart.

He thinks at every step that someone will see and ask him what he is doing, but not a single person notices. Part of him dances with glee and part of him screams with despair. He is an invisible man.

The suitcases go on next. He has left it for far too long, and the ones at the bottom of the pile collapse when he tries to take them out. Pieces of rotten flesh wash out onto the floor, along with maggots and flies in large numbers. He does what he can to clean it up, and hopes an old car tyre will take the blame for the smell that lingers.

No one has stirred in the gardens next door. At last, the bonfire is ready. He sets it alight.

Even though the fire burns hot and bright, Des feels cold to the bone. He sweats nervously as children come to look at the flames, warning them not to get too close. He almost wishes they would dance like devils around the funeral pyre, sending those lost souls on their way to Valhalla or whatever awaits them.

As the sparks fly into the air, someone in a nearby home plays *Tubular Bells* with the windows open.

Des watches the bodies mingling with one another to become the same pile of ashes, and he thinks of the souls of the men, the men who were inside the bodies. He wonders if the sparks are their souls flying out, released at last.

All of a sudden, he knows. He feels it inside, the fire calling to him in a way that he cannot describe. The fire and the music. The souls escaped long ago. They live now inside him, all of them, their souls and fates taken in and interwoven with his own.

There could be no funeral for these men. No uniform cemetery with its strangely anonymous headstones. No forgetting, no real loss. They are inside him now, preserved, continuing. They will be a single unity of ash, and inside him there is a single unity of souls.

The children go home. Des stays to watch, drinking a bottle of beer and weeping.

He has killed six men. He has cut them into pieces. He has burned them right in the open, in front of the whole neighbourhood, and not a single person has noticed.

Des wonders how all of this could be possible. How he, a normal man, a soldier, a Civil Service man, a Scot, a Union man, could have done all of this.

He wonders when he will wake up from this bad dream.

He goes inside, returning occasionally to check the bones and stir them over. He uses a garden rake to crush a skull and comb it into the ashes as powder.

He dumps the spare bricks on top of the ashes when the fire is all gone, and disinfects the shed. He does not, and he knows he will not, wake up from the dream.

"It's alright," he tells Bleep, once he is inside again. "Everything's alright now."

The dog whimpers and leans against his leg, looking up at him with sorrowful eyes.

Chapter Twenty-Two

Everything has been cleansed from him. Now he carries more souls than his own, and the rest of it has been washed away. Des feels like a great weight has been taken off his shoulders. He can be a normal citizen again. A reasonable person, with no need to hide.

He goes to the Salisbury again. One of his favourite haunts. There he meets a man. They talk with a twinkling in their eyes. When the man suggests going somewhere else, Des has no hesitation.

His hands have been wiped clean. When he brings this man with a twinkle in his eye back to Melrose Avenue, he has no fear that the man will leave. Of course, he will leave. In the morning, when all is concluded, he will leave – and that is right, and natural. There is no problem with this, not anymore.

They have sex. The first time in so long. Des sleeps soundly with the other man next to him, and feels a gentle sense of satisfaction when he waves him off at the train station the next morning. He feels like the dark part of him might be gone for good.

January feels like a real new start. 1981 is here and moods are changing, as they always seem to.

Des strolls the streets of Soho until he comes to the Golden Lion, and heads in for a drink. Why not? He's a free man living in a free country.

At the end of the night, a fellow Scot challenges him to a drinking contest. He mentions that he is 18 and yet has been drinking since long before he came of legal drinking age. He has experience despite his youth, he points out. Laughing, Des agrees.

"You're on," he says, knowing that he will win.

The Scot has blue eyes, bright blue eyes that really seem to fix into him. He is wearing a green tracksuit top and trainers, though he doesn't exactly look the sporty type. He is slim and attractive; the kind of guy Des wouldn't mind having a drinking contest with at any time.

Of course, it helps that he's a Scot.

They head back to the flat to continue their drinking.

End of the night; end of drinking; end of person. How neat and tidy.

Somehow, the shades slip down again, and Des is no longer fresh and new, no longer free and clear, no longer safe. He is back in the bad dream again.

Des wakes up in the morning and feels his skull tight inside his head, last night's drink still thick on him. The flat is littered with empty cans and abandoned glasses, and even items of clothing strewn across the floor. He gets down from the bed and sits in his chair, and tries to make sense of the scene.

There is a dead body lying on the floor in front of him.

Bleep trots over, looking for reassurance.

"Everything's alright, weed," he says, scratching her behind her ears. She wags her tail at that and seems happy enough.

Des gets up from the chair and kneels beside the body instead, and is almost surprised to find that his hands are shaking. He reaches over to the body's neck and pulls off the tie which is wrapped tightly around it.

The face is puffed out and red, the eyes piercing blue no longer. Des rolls him onto his back and he makes a noise like a sigh as the last air leaves his lungs. Des stares at the body for a long while, smoking a cigarette with shaking hands.

Hell, fucking hell, how long can this go on and on? he thinks. He didn't even give this one a proper ritual. It is still lying where he left it in the night, unwashed and unclaimed. He doesn't even know if he is doing it for the fantasy anymore, or if he is on autopilot, destroying everything he can get his hands upon.

He picks up Bleep, by now no longer wagging her tail. She has picked up on his distress and is looking at him mournfully, trying to find a way to be useful to her master.

"Bleep, what's going to become of us?" he says out loud, cradling her in his arms. Once he speaks, it feels like he can't stop. "Who will look after you when they come for me? They're all gone, one after the other, it was me, me, nobody else but me… This is all my work. I must be mad, insane. They're dead forever by these hands."

He cries until he starts to feel angry. Then, full of self-loathing and righteous rage, he overturns the coffee table in one sharp movement. Everything on it crashes to the floor, and he buries his head in his hands for a moment as Bleep scurries out of reach.

Then he finds another target, his union correspondence all preserved in a neat plastic folder, and throws that across the room. It strikes the playing arm that has been poised over the LP turning silently all night. The music starts to play and it drowns out all of his other thoughts, until he is left staring at the wreckage on the floor, feeling empty.

At last the music has a cleansing effect, bringing him back to reality. He cannot sit and stare, or throw a rage tantrum, forever. Something has to be done before he can move forward.

Eventually, he gets to work and cleans up the body. He thinks about the people who live upstairs and finds he does not care at all what they think about all the noise. He will make as much noise as he wants. This, he hopes, is the last one.

Chapter Twenty-Three

It is 1955. Ten-year-old Dennis is playing on his own near a disused toilet when an opportunity strikes.

He has been wondering about it for some time, but now he decides to act upon his childish imaginings. He wants to see what will happen. He wants to know what it looks like when something goes to that 'better place' that everyone is always talking about.

There is a friendly neighbourhood cat, perhaps a stray, that he has seen and petted often. It doesn't seem to worry about coming with him into the building, which is some stroke of luck. If the cat wasn't willing, Dennis wasn't about to force it and win himself a face full of scratches.

It is so trusting that it barely even reacts when he slips a wire around its neck. It probably feels just like a collar going on there.

The wire is attached to the cistern pipe, and when he pulls it up, the cat rises sharply into the air.

Now it struggles; it does not have the air to yowl, but it claws at the space around it as if it might lash out and attack the invisible force holding it by the neck. Des steps back sharply so that it cannot possibly reach him, though he still holds tightly to the wire.

A cat is a small thing; it does not struggle for long, and then it is done. It hangs there lifeless, swinging back and forwards slightly under the momentum of its last movements.

Dennis pokes the dead cat and then moves back as if he has been stung. It is disgusting, all of it is disgusting. How can he have been so cruel to the poor thing? True, he wanted to see the process of killing a cat, and to know what it was like. The dead cat itself, though, is an unfortunate by-product that he would have liked to avoid if it were possible. Swinging there, now, it is a thing that he regrets deeply.

It holds no interest to him, so he turns away. He thinks about the time he found his pet pigeon killed by some older boys, and how he had cried and cried. He wonders if the cat has an owner and instantly feels ashamed. It was a cruel thing he had done, that was for certain.

He decided to bury it down deep, to forget about it, and never broach the subject again if he could. He knew what it was like to kill a cat now, and he knew that it was a horrible, disgusting, cruel thing. There would be no need for any further experiments on the subject.

That shame, he could already tell, would be hanging on his shoulders forever.

Chapter Twenty-Four

Des meets a boy from Belfast wandering around the West End. He likes the ones that wander. Usually, they have no one waiting for them. Nowhere to go. That makes them more compliant, more agreeable; more likely to agree with him when he delivers his sermons on the importance of the workforce.

This Belfast boy can't be 25 yet, a tall lad who gamely drinks with him in a string of pubs before they go home. The February air is a lot less cold when you have a few drinks inside of you.

Des wakes up in the morning and catches sight of his tie dangling off the side of a chair, and instantly he knows what he has done. Sure enough, there is a body on the floor, next to the coffee table.

He groans to himself and puts it into the cupboard, cleaning up a little around the place, throwing away empty beer cans and washing empty glasses. He will deal with the body later. For now, he needs to get dressed and go to work.

When he comes home from work in the evening, he opens the cupboard to put his coat away and is startled to see the body waiting there. He had quite forgotten about it.

He puts it under the floorboards now, adding a few more deodorant sticks along with it. Soon the flies will start to come out again in the summer months. What he will do then, he does not want to think about.

Chapter Twenty-Five

After he dyed his hair blond, Des thought that he looked like the pretty ideal. Aryan. Youthful. Younger than his own years. That was a real kick, seeing himself like that in the mirror.

What really caught his attention that winter, though, was the gorilla.

Working as a security guard, he is posted to the Natural History Museum, patrolling their warehouse. There are so many incredible things inside that warehouse. Most interesting of all, however, is the gorilla.

It is real, and stuffed. It has false eyes but somehow it still looks so alive. So powerful. He feels a shiver run through him when he stands in front of it. He thinks about the contrast between the big, black, strong gorilla, and himself: young, blond, defenceless against such a creature. He thinks about King Kong and Fay Wray.

His heart starts to beat harder and faster until it is the only thing he can hear. He continues to stare at the gorilla even though his heart is pumping so hard it feels as though it will tear out of his chest. At last, he can't hold back. He has to do something.

He strips off his own clothes hurriedly, right there in the warehouse. Good thing it is his job to keep others out. He won't be disturbed by anyone else. It is so arousing to be naked there, in front of the gorilla, to have its eyes on him.

He steps forward until the gorilla's arm is in the right place, until it can touch his own naked skin. He imagines looking down at the pair of them from above, how they must look: the youth about to be carried off to the gorilla's jungle lair.

He is starting to really get carried away when he glances down. All at once, everything deflates. The gorilla has a pathetic little stump for a penis, nothing at all to write home about. Nothing manly or strong about that.

Des sighs, and puts his clothes back on.

This is no way to spend the nights, he thinks. That's when he decides to get a new job, so he can go out to pubs at night instead and meet young gay men, and live the life he wants to have.

Chapter Twenty-Six

Another pub. Leaning up against the bar in a venue in Soho that is known for the gay crowd, Des assesses the room casually. There are one or two likely types here, but he's in no rush. Let them come to him, he thinks.

"You look a little lonely," someone says at his right elbow.

Des turns to see a young man with a broad smile and tousled brown hair. He adjusts his stance to face the man, finding him interesting all of a sudden. "Mebbe," he replies. "I'm just waiting for somebody to help fix that."

The young man grins further, and leans on the bar next to him. "Maybe I can give it a try," he says. "Alex."

"Des," he replies, nodding. "Let's see what you've got, then, Alex."

"I always find a good start is having a drink in hand," he says, nodding at Des' empty pint glass. "What are you drinking?"

"Allow me," Des says, shaking his head. He likes to be the one buying the drinks, doing the favours. It puts him in control.

They take their drinks over to a table which has just been vacated, sliding into the spot before someone else can take advantage of the rare opportunity in the crowded bar. They chit-chat for a while; Alex is flirtatious and manages to fit in an innuendo or a sly reference every other sentence, which Des at least finds amusing. When some men do it, they come across as sleazy. For others, it just makes them sound like idiots. Alex manages to make it charming.

The barman rings a bell loudly from the side of the bar, and everyone groans audibly. Last orders; time to clear out. Des drains his pint and puts the glass down onto the table decisively.

"Right," he says. "Seems like it's time to get out of here."

"What a shame," Alex says, putting his own empty glass down. "Just when I was starting to enjoy myself."

"I'm heading back to my flat, if you want to join me," Des says, a little bit of a twinkle in his eye. After all, this does seem like a sure thing.

"Why not?" Alex agrees. "We can carry on our chat there."

"And get some more booze on the way, of course," Des winks, getting up and grabbing his coat.

The two of them make their way outside and start to walk. The tube; the off-license; the long walk home.

As they progress more and more into the residential territory, where it is less busy and there is hardly anyone to see them on the street, Alex gets more and more flirty. He winds up stopping Des in the street to nuzzle at his neck, slipping his hands inside Des' coat. Des leans away and makes a sound of disapproval low in his throat. He doesn't want to be carrying on like this in public.

"What's wrong?" Alex asks, sounding a little hurt. He has the look about him of a man whose mood could turn on a sixpence.

"There's no need for that, out here," Des says reprovingly, gesturing at the nearby houses as if to emphasise that they are outside.

"Are you ashamed of it?" Alex asks, his voice rising in volume. "Ashamed of who you are? Are you one of them?"

"I'm not ashamed," Des retorts, half-incredulously. "I just prefer to have my fun in private."

Alex snorts derisively. "Yeah, I'm sure," he says, fully on the attack now. "You'll have me in bed all night getting your kicks and then throw me out in the morning before everyone else wakes up, is that it?"

"You can leave whatever time you like," Des says, his eyes narrowed. He is almost done with this youth. "But all I want to do in bed tonight is sleep."

"So, I'm wasting my time completely, then," Alex sums up. If he was unrestrained by the general laws of physics and possibility, Des thinks, Alex would probably spew fire from his eyes right now.

"I guess you are," Des says. He knows now that this night is going nowhere. They'll have no quiet drinking in front of the TV, no shared music, no gentle caressing and heavy sleep. There's no point in trying to convince Alex otherwise when the reward won't even be worth it.

Alex turns on his heel and storms off, back in the direction of the tube, landing a few choice epithets and curses over his shoulder as he goes.

Des stands in the middle of the street, and looks down at the bag of supplies in his hand. A little aimless, toting all of this beer around when he only wants the Bacardi and coke. A waste of a night, indeed. Looks like he will be drinking and feeling lonely after all; no change from a few hours ago, almost as if nothing happened in the interim. Almost, but worse. He turns around, but Alex is already only a small blob far off at the end of the road, just about to disappear from sight completely.

Des shrugs his shoulders and walks home. Nothing else for it but that.

Chapter Twenty-Seven

A bar in August. Drink in hand, Des is talking to a couple of men, telling them about the government and how they repress the proletariat and we would all be better off without their interference. He feels like he is in prime flow, really going for it. Everything he says has a ring of truth, and he feels a righteousness in his delivery.

At least, that's how he feels. The men seem disinterested in what he has to say. First, they start looking down into their glasses more and more rather than at him. Then, they start glancing around at the rest of the room idly. Gradually, they stop replying to his words with full sentences, and then they stop even grunting or nodding. They start to exchange glances with one another, and openly stare around the rest of the room as if searching for something.

"Sorry," one of them says, all of a sudden, cutting him off mid-sentence. "I've just seen an old friend."

He gets up and leaves, without any more of an explanation than that. The man left behind gapes after him, his face a mask of betrayal. He glances back at Des, who clears his throat.

"As I was saying," he begins, but the other man cuts him off.

"Actually, sorry, I just need to go to the loo," he says, hurriedly. He gets up, leaving a quarter of his pint behind. "Uh, see you later," he adds at the last minute, hovering over the table before bolting away.

Des sighs. He drains his own glass and looks around the pub. The first man who escaped is very obviously trying to chat up a stranger, and the second one will be doing the same when he gets out of the loo.

There is nothing for Des here tonight. It happens; you can't always get lucky. It's just a shame how it feels when he heads back to the flat without anyone else by his side, sitting down with Bleep in front of the television and feeling suddenly incredibly isolated in contrast to the crowded bars.

He gets up and puts on his coat, and leaves. Time for the journey home. Even if it will be a lonely one, and even if a small dog and loneliness are the only things waiting for him there, it is a journey that still has to be made.

Chapter Twenty-Eight

Des gets up on Thursday the 17th of September just as he has done on every working day for a good long while. He wakes, prepares himself for work, and dresses in a pair of dark trousers with a blue shirt. He adds his customary blue tie, puts on his shoes, and slips into his pale grey tweed jacket. Ready to go, he adjusts his rimless spectacles and runs a hand through his thick, brown hair to ensure it is in place.

He glances a farewell to Bleep and heads outside, walking down Melrose Avenue on his way to the tube station just as he always does.

Usually, however, there is no young man slumped against the garden wall of a neighbour. This development, being rather out of the ordinary, stops him in his tracks.

Des glances behind himself quickly; there is no one else around. It seems like the onus is on him to be community spirited. It will mean being late for work, but he stops to check anyway.

"Are you alright?" he asks, the question perhaps a stupid one.

"Yeah," the young man manages, looking up. His face is pale. "It's my epilepsy pills. They make my legs go a bit funny."

"You should have someone professional look at you," Des pronounces sagely, looking him over.

The young man shrugs. "I don't know," he admits, shivering a little in the cold air.

Des glances back down the road; there's still only himself around to lend a hand. "Come back to my flat and sit down," he said. "At least just for a coffee."

The young man agrees and starts struggling to push himself upright, so Des leans down and offers him a shoulder. He helps him the short distance down the road, though it is a challenge to move even that short distance; the man's legs keep giving way, and he is obviously feeling faint and dizzy from the way that he sways around.

Finally having deposited him in an armchair, Des pours them both a coffee. The office will have to wait.

"What's your name?" he asks, putting a hot cup down on the coffee table. "I'm Des, by the way."

"Malcolm," he says. There's a pause as he thinks about it, then he adds, "Malcolm Barlow. Just in case."

"Just in case, what?"

"In case I have a fit or something and you need to tell the ambulance who I am."

That gives Des pause. He is increasingly uneasy about this. There's work to be done at the office, and besides, this Malcolm does not look healthy at all. He looks like he could collapse at any given second. Does he really want that going on in his house?

Des directs a glance towards his own floorboards. Underneath is a horror that only he knows about, and he needs it to stay that way. He has managed to restrain himself since the early part of the year and now that 1981 is coming to a close, the heat and stink of the summer gone, he does not want any risk of discovery before the year is out. That would be cruel indeed, to be caught only when he seems at last to have reached some kind of drought in his violence.

A doctor and policeman coming into the house at the same time to investigate a death might recognise the smell that most other people simply pass off as musty. They might have come across bodies left to rot for months before. But if he can head this off at the pass, get a couple of paramedics who want to be in and out quickly with their patient instead of a detective who will linger, he might survive.

"I'm going up to call an ambulance," he decides, getting out of his chair.

"Haven't you got a phone?" Malcolm asks, glancing around dubiously.

"It's disconnected," Des tells him brusquely, grabbing his jacket up again. "Not to worry. It's only Kendal Avenue I need to go to for the phone box."

"I'll come, then," Malcolm says, making to get up even though his voice is faint and distant.

"No, no," Des says hastily, thinking about the toil of half-carrying him all the way to the box. "You stay here and... look after Bleep. My dog."

Bleep sits up and wags her tail at the mention of her name, and Malcolm acquiesces. He sinks back into the cushions of the chair quietly, content to wait now.

Des curses himself roundly all the way to the phone box. Why did he have to go and get involved with this lad? Still, once he gets the ambulance round, Malcolm will be out of his hair. Then he can get back to work and thrill them all with his tale of a good deed done. All in all, it might not turn out so badly.

It only takes ten minutes for the ambulance to come; with his walk back to the house included in that time, he doesn't have to put up with the weak and pale Malcolm for long at all. The paramedics whisk him off to the Park Royal Hospital, information Des neither wants nor needs but is given all the same, and he finally manages to get his journey to work underway.

Chapter Twenty-Nine

Friday comes, and Des is glad of an uninterrupted journey to work this time. He spends the day filling his duties as he always does, organising a little paperwork for the CPSA, and sharing a few dark jokes with his co-workers. Several of them are being a little nicer to him than usual, having heard about how heroic he was to rescue a young epileptic man on the street the day before.

The shine is already starting to wear off, though, since the story involved no blood or jumping into icy rivers or selfless sacrifice, as the best hero stories do. Never mind; it was nice for a moment or two.

He heads out of the office at 5.30pm and gets on the tube to go home, feeling a little lighter with the knowledge that the weekend is ahead. Des is content to get home, walk Bleep, eat some food, and watch television with a drink or two until he falls asleep.

The second that he sees Malcolm Barlow sitting on his doorstep, he watches those plans start to crumble into dust.

"You're supposed to be in hospital," he says, almost accusatory. His good deed has won him a little nicety, and he does not like the thought of it being undone so quickly.

"I'm alright now," Malcolm says, getting up and brushing dirt off the seat of his jeans. "I was discharged. I didn't know where else to go."

"So, you came to me?" Des asks.

"Thought I'd better say thanks for yesterday," Malcolm shrugs. "Got a bit lost though. Thought it was 295 you lived at, and I was wandering up and down the street. I guessed you were at work, when I figured out the right number, so I waited for you to get back."

"Well, you'd better come in then," Des says, suppressing a theatrical sigh. This is a nuisance. He wants to follow his normal routine; this boy wants to disrupt it. What is he after, anyway? A free meal and a bed for the night, no doubt. You do one act of kindness and people think you've turned into a charity.

Des decides to follow his own routine all the same. This boy can't disrupt him; he has plans. He cooks himself some food and resolutely sits down in front of the television with a Bacardi and coke. This night will go how he wants it to, Malcolm or no Malcolm.

"Can I have one?" Malcolm asks.

Des looks over and sees Malcolm's eyes trained on the Bacardi and coke. "Won't that be a problem? With your pills?"

"No, it's fine, promise," Malcolm grins. "I do it all the time."

Des sighs, and gets up. "Be it on your own head," he says, reaching for the Bacardi bottle.

They have two drinks before Malcolm falls unconscious.

Looking at him, Des feels a peculiar mix of feelings. Most of all, he feels annoyed. The walk to the phone box in the cold night is not going to be a fun one. Besides which, he is settled now and comfortable. He has had his drinks, his food, his television; the next step is supposed to be going to sleep.

There is that same old worry, too, niggling away in the back of his mind. There is that fusty smell about the flat which most people probably put down to the aroma of a bachelor living on his own. But it is not. It is the smell of death coming up from the floorboards. The kind of smell a seasoned police officer will recognise. He can picture it so clearly in his head.

If he calls the ambulance, and they don't recognise the smell, what next? The police coming to investigate? Asking him questions, maybe even thinking that he gave Malcolm the drink on purpose to make him pass out? He thinks back to the times the police have been by in the past, and how he laughed things off as domestic arguments. They accepted his bluffing then, but this one could be a little trickier. He's not sure he will be able to make it sound so casual.

Yes, officer, I allowed him to have a drink even though I knew he was on medication, he thinks to himself. *Oh, no, I didn't think it would have any effect.*

It sounds hollow even inside his own mind. Of course he suspected that something like this might happen; he simply hadn't cared.

He debates for twenty minutes or so as his programme ends. After that, something must be done.

He gets up and walks over to Malcolm, places his hands around his neck, and squeezes as hard as he can.

He stays that way for two, perhaps three minutes; he knows this is the most convenient thing to do. There won't be any more hassle tonight if he does it this way.

When he feels that it has been long enough, Des lets go of the neck and walks back to his chair. There doesn't seem to be any point in checking for a pulse. The boy was half dead already. He finishes off his drink, switches off the television, and gets into bed.

In the morning, he can hardly be bothered to deal with the body. He puts it into the cupboard under the sink. He will pry up the floorboards later, when he works up the energy to care.

Chapter Thirty

In 1973 he was training to be a police officer. He remembers that spring well, because it was the first time that he really began to think that he might have something wrong in his head.

He passes his exams and gets posted to Willesden Green on probation. His first assignment is to work the morgue. He and a group of others are given a briefing in the corridor of the building, told what to expect and braced as much as possible. Then they are sent in, three at a time, to see their first dead bodies.

Except that this is not the first time for Des. He has seen it all on patrol in Aden; exploded bodies lying on the sides of the road, bits of themselves everywhere. A few tame old murders can't do anything for him. Even seeing them cut open for the post-mortem leaves him unaffected.

The other trainees have to go and be sick. Des stays to look.

There is a young girl on one of the slabs. She is only twelve years old. Her body is smooth and slim, and she has blonde hair. She looks almost like she could be a little boy.

The morgue assistant is an old man with a slight hunchback, perhaps developed from wheeling around the dead for so many years. He moves the slab on wheels, and as he does so, the girl's hand flops out.

Des instantly feels himself growing hard.

He looks away, but even so, his mind continues. He thinks about the disgusting, disfigured old man having his way with the smooth, pure, and passive body. He imagines a young boy left at the mercy of an old man who can do whatever he likes. Even when he leaves the room, he has to fight hard to keep the fantasy at bay.

That is when he knows there is something wrong with him.

Chapter Thirty-One

Finally, it's time to move on.

The last few months have not been good for him. It all started with a letter at work; he had wanted to go to the Overseas Workers Section, but the panel decided that he was not eligible.

They said that his manner with his colleagues was 'usually outspoken and often overbearing'. Apparently, they could not risk the idea that he might act this way with the public too. Outspoken and overbearing – what a ridiculous thing for them to say. So many times, he has noticed that speaking his mind seems to count as a black mark against his name. Now this – this is a real smear on his character.

Glancing around the office after he reads the letter, he wonders which of his colleagues ratted him out. Which of them spoke badly about him when they were asked. Which of them betrayed him.

That was bad enough. He had started drinking more and more, staying out late and then stumbling in to work in the morning. He was inviting men back without even thinking about it, almost recklessly. So many of them passed through his home without a moment's disturbance. He hoped they thought him good company.

One night, though, a trip to the Cricklewood Arms proves fateful.

After he leaves the pub, walking home, someone approaches him fast and shoves something sharp into his face, warning him not to fight. They take his wallet, his favourite jacket, and even his shoes. There was £300 in the wallet; a month's full wages. He curses himself for carrying it all around like that. He stumbles home on cold and injured feet, wincing at every sharp stone lying on the pavement.

It does not stop him. He is on some kind of collision course, almost addicted to the recklessness of his life. Part of him wonders if he brings so many worthless men back with him because he is waiting to see which of them he will kill.

But he is not always the predator; sometimes, he, too, can be a victim. One opportunist wakes before him and steals out of the flat with his movie camera and projector. He loved that camera. He loved watching back his movies. The fact that someone could take it from under his nose is almost too much to bear.

He remembers shouting at Twinkle for letting someone steal from them, and wonders what Twinkle would think if he saw him now.

Some weeks later, he is walking to work when he feels a sharp pain in his chest at the end of Melrose Avenue. He collapses, but drags himself up to his feet, desperate to get to the phone box. When he manages to stagger there and call the ambulance, he tells them to come fast: with the pain in his chest and the struggle to breathe, he knows that he is having a heart attack.

The wait for the paramedics to come is one of the longest he has ever endured. He feels the pain of his heart swelling in his chest and wonders if they will die before they get to him.

That, he knows, would be disastrous. They would go into his house to clear up his things and they would notice. They would find out. They would discover one body after another and everyone would know what he has done. He thinks of the families, waiting to hear about their beloved son; the pain and anger that they will feel. He imagines a future where they suffer through this without even being able to see justice, because he died from a heart attack, and his heart squeezes tighter and tighter.

When they finally come, he wishes he had never called them in the first place.

It is not a heart attack. That news is humiliating enough. It seems it was simply stress and exhaustion that brought him to his knees. He makes up some story about being under pressure at work. Well, in a way, he is. They don't need to know that the disposal of bodies is the thing stressing him out the most.

In the end, though, it is not this incident, or any that came before it, that finally brings him to realise that Melrose Avenue is no longer his home. It is the landlord, who is constantly trying to force him out.

Des is no conspiracy theorist, but this time he knows for certain that the landlord is out to get him. There are foreign men waiting outside his house a couple of times who demand to inspect his flat without giving the proper notice period; they are threatening and vulgar. He takes this as an intimidation tactic and complains about it to Ellis & Co.

It turns out that there have been some complaints about Des already, from the other residents. They aren't happy that he plays his music at all hours, or that he has men coming over, different men every week. They don't like seeing men slink outside in the morning wearing last night's clothes. They don't like, he reads between the lines, having to live near a gay man. Most of all, they don't like the smell that comes from his rooms.

Then, perhaps because he had been told to relent, the landlord takes things up a gear. He hires someone to come and vandalise the whole flat. The whole flat!

When he arrives home from work, the door is hanging on its hinges, clearly open. He steps inside with his heart hammering fast. Many thoughts flash through his head: a family member who somehow knows and wants revenge, a burglary, a police raid, the foreign men come to carry out their unworded threats. He steps through into the flat and gazes around in horror.

Everything he owns is smashed or covered with creosote. All of it, ruined: his record player, his collection of records, his clothes. Everything but the suit he walked home in.

He literally has nothing. All of these years of building up a life; building a record collection; buying clothes and pieces of furniture one by one. All of those months of earnings – all gone in one moment. Barely anything is salvageable, and even those things that are have been damaged in some way.

Starting from zero again is a kind of terrifying prospect, but at least the men didn't want to damage their employer's property. They didn't try to rip up the floorboards. That is one small mercy.

Having no one else to tell about it, he complains to his colleagues about what happened, and there is one unexpected ray of goodness that moves him almost to tears. A couple of weeks after the incident, one of his co-workers presents him with a cheque for £85, apparently achieved with a whip-round of the office. He is humbled; brought to his knees by something entirely different, this time. Too choked to thank them in person, he instead writes an eloquent letter of thanks to the whole team.

He believes that this is the very milk of human kindness. This is that mystical property that so many have written about. The ability to support a fellow man in his hour of need. Despite all of his preaching about brotherhood and solidarity, he has never been able to make a gesture as beautiful as this one.

Rays of goodness aside, it is clear that he must move on. So, move on, he does.

When everything is settled for the move, there's only one more thing to take care of. He brings out the bodies from under the floorboards: the Scot, the Belfast boy, and Malcolm Barlow. He has started to cut them up a few times in the past few months, but never quite finished the job; it is nasty work, and the part of it all that he cares for the least.

Well, it's time for it now, and if he doesn't get it done then there will be no way to get rid of them. He lays them out on the floor and kneels in solemn reverence, despite the overwhelmingly awful smell.

He holds his breath as much as he can and masturbates while they lay on the floor next to him, a final farewell to show them how much he appreciates them. His way of saying a few words over the bodies, he supposes.

That done, he puts Bleep outside and drinks as much Bacardi as he is able to without passing out, and cuts them up into chunks so they will fit on the fire easier.

It is gruesome work. The flesh has steadily been decaying in its packages and under the floorboards, and the stench is overpowering. Many times, he has to stop to throw up, even when he is so drunk he barely even knows who he is anymore. He simply drinks a little more to get through it.

He cannot stand the sight of it all, and he begins to feel half-mad. But the task must be completed, or it has all been a waste of time. The logic part of his brain takes over, instructing him to do *this* part next and then move on to *that* part after, as if he is doing nothing more unusual than filling in a form at work. Wrapping his brain in the instructional side of the work like that helps him forget, for a few moments here and there, what it is that he is doing.

He finally gets them into small enough pieces that he can wrap them up into new, smaller packages and place them under the floorboards again. That just leaves the entrails: a bag of viscera, sloppy and disgusting, smelling worse than any of it.

Near the end of the garden is his little space to leave the soft entrails out for all the wee wild beasties to eat, and they will surely have their fill of it tonight. But three men produce a lot of viscera. Even with the space filled, that still leaves a whole carrier bag of the stuff, far too much to go unnoticed even if he emptied it right on top of the rest.

Des is drunk; too drunk to think properly. Bleep needs a walk, so he takes her out with the bag of viscera still in his hand. It stinks every time he moves his arm, the wet and dark contents slopping around or sticking to the sides as the smell wafts up.

They reach Gladstone Park, where Bleep likes to have her daily romp around, and Des is tired of carrying it around. He simply puts it down at the side of the road, as if it were a bag of Bleep's droppings scooped up off the pavement. His fingerprints are all over it, but he is too drunk to be really concerned.

In consequent days he will worry about the bag, and the evidence it represented; but no one ever comes knocking on his door. Although it is undoubtedly found by someone and removed, it seems that no one could mentally connect this dark and melting pile of innards with a murder. Much more comfortable for them to imagine that it comes from a cow, or a dog, or a pig. Another lucky break given by the apathy of human thought.

Des builds the bonfire the morning before he is due to leave, and sets it ablaze while he packs up the rest of his belongings. Neighbours assume he is just clearing out his broken and smashed possessions so that he does not need to move with them. Just like that, another three bodies gone up in smoke.

23 Cranley Gardens will be his next home. Though he is to share the flat with a number of other tenants, he will be on the top floor, and with no private access to the garden. Perhaps this will be the new start that he needs. Perhaps this time, he can really stop.

Chapter Thirty-Two

Cranley Gardens is, it seems, a much nicer neighbourhood than his last. On top of that, Des is feeling more sociable lately, and the tube is closer by. He has friends over to stay, real friends, and he enjoys their company. He finds himself feeling a lot more relaxed. The demons of Melrose Avenue are behind him.

His fellow tenants seem nice enough, though he doesn't talk with them much; just enough, he hopes, to keep them onside. After all, if the tenants in his last house had not complained about him so much, perhaps the landlord would not have given him the push.

There is Fiona downstairs, and her boyfriend Jim, who is somewhat annoying but probably harmless. There is Vivienne and Monique, a Kiwi and a Dutch girl, the most unusual of combinations. The middle floor is unoccupied, which Des enjoys very much. It means a barrier of sound between above and below, even though he does not anticipate making much noise here. It gives that little bit more privacy when he brings men home, which he has at last begun to do with a more selective process.

The other tenants work just as he does, so they barely see each other. There is only the occasional passing and greeting on the stairs or at the front door. That cannot be avoided, it seems, though they never seem to want to socialise with him any further. He does not mind about this. The fact that he has a new home, and a more hospitable one at that, is enough to keep him satisfied.

There is also a ray of light in his work life. His long-delayed promotion has at last been granted. He is proud to call himself an executive officer – finally! After so many years of waiting and expecting, they have given him what he deserves. He cannot describe how happy he is to have his skill and experience recognised.

The only catch is that there is no position for an executive officer available at Denmark Street, and so he must move on. He is posted to the Kentish Town branch, which comes almost as a welcome change. No one knows who he is here, or has a pre-supposed idea of what he is about. When he walks by someone's desk and tries to strike up a conversation, people don't hold up books or newspapers in front of their faces to pretend they are busy. It's nice to feel like a human again.

His boss is Janet, a wonderful woman who he warms to immediately. Des is determined to do well here and show his worth, and perhaps prove that he is ready to go even further. He declines to take his leave for the year and throws himself into the job as much as possible, volunteering to stay late and take on extra work.

One night comes when he realises that he really has found a much better working home than his last. He stays to help out well past home time, giving Janet a hand so that she does not have to stay even later. A flood has battered through their office and left a mess behind, and he is the only one from the whole team who stays behind to help mop up. He finds that a bit of an impertinence; they all have to work in the office, after all, whether it is cleaned up or not.

Janet buys him a pack of cigarettes to thank him for helping out, and it warms his heart in a way that he has not felt in years. Receiving a gift is such a small thing, but it is remarkable how much you miss it when you never receive any. To be recognised and thought of – and to be given something that he likes and wants – is an incredible thing. He is astonished at the gesture, and blown away. One thing is for sure. From that day, he knows he will be loyal to whatever she requires him to do. She is the kind of leader he can get behind.

These small moments light up his world in a way that makes everything seem so much better than before. He is still attempting to replace the furniture he has lost; it is an uphill struggle, a battle to save enough for each piece. The flat may seem spartan, but at least he is getting somewhere. That is the most important thing.

Then comes November, and a trip to the Golden Lion in Soho, one of his preferred haunts. Des likes to prop up the bar here, and sometimes chat to others, and sometimes even find someone to take home.

He watches over the top of his pint as a young man sitting on the other end of the bar is approached by another, the two of them engaging in a brief conversation. The one sitting down seems uninterested in what the other is saying, but he won't go away. He keeps talking at him, trying to touch him, even. Des can't hear what they are saying, but there's a lot of head-shaking going on from the sitting man. There's a lot of insistent and aggressive body language on the other side.

He narrows his eyes, frowns, and gets up with his pint in hand.

"Hey, you," he says, abandoning politeness in the face of the circumstances. The aggressor turns around.

"You got a problem, mate?" he sneers.

"I don't think my boyfriend is interested," Des replies, with a raised eyebrow.

The aggressor looks between the two of them briefly, and the sitting man has enough sense to play along at least to the extent of not raising any suspicions. He even smiles warmly at Des, as if they know each other.

After a moment, the harasser throws his hands up in the air and backs away to find someone else to hassle.

"Thanks," the young man at the bar says, giving Des a grateful look. "I didn't think he was ever going to go away."

"Aye, no problem," Des replies. "I could see him from over there. Looked like he wasn't taking no for an answer."

"You're right there," the man says, shaking his head. "I'm Paul. Can I buy you a drink to say thanks?"

"Sure," Des says, swiftly dispatching of his own and placing the empty glass down on the bar with a satisfied panache. "I never turn down a free pint."

"You sound a lot like myself," Paul laughs, gesturing to the barman to pour them another couple of the same.

They get on well. Paul has dark, thick, curly hair which puts him right up Des' street, not to mention his appealing height and build. Des knows what he likes, and Paul fits the bill. It's a good job he intervened, really. Gives them an excuse to talk – a way to break the ice.

After a couple of drinks, Des introduces the idea of a stroll back to his flat for a few more drinks that will, of course, cost significantly less.

Paul agrees, on the condition that they watch *Panorama*.

He is shaping up to be Des' kind of guy in all sorts of ways.

They make a genial time out of it, watching the television with snacks and Bacardi. Des fires out a few of his snappy remarks about the presenters or the topics, and Paul laughs.

They watch the *Nine O'Clock News* together and Paul realises how late it is. He has to let his mother know that he won't be home until later, so he goes to the payphone in the hall and gives her a call.

Inside, Des waits with the television for company. He pours another drink so that it will be ready when Paul comes back in.

After an hour, Paul comes to a realisation. "I'm pretty drunk," he says, announcing the news like a grave declaration of the previously unknown.

Des nods, and raises his glass in salute, grinning wide. "I'm with you, there," he agrees.

"Don't think I'll be able to make it back," Paul says, continuing the thought.

"Ah, don't worry about it," Des says dismissively. "There's room at the inn. I'll not kick you out. You can sleep in my bed."

"What about you?" Paul asks, a little tentatively.

"I can sleep in my bed too," Des says grandly, taking another swig from his Bacardi and coke.

Paul almost leaps out of the chair, swaying desperately and clutching onto the arm to steady himself after the initial burst of excitement, and goes to call his mother again. He won't be going home tonight. Although it's a little sad to see a grown man calling his mother all of the time and stuck under her thumb like that, but each to his own, Des thinks. At least he has someone waiting at home to call.

Des finishes his drink and Paul stretches and yawns, a fair imitation of a tired man from a drunk one.

"Bed time," Des says, planting his empty glass on the coffee table and shepherding him through to the other room.

Once they are in bed, Paul is clearly not as tired as he pretended. He starts with a nuzzling, a light graze of a hand, and before long it turns to caressing. It is obvious to any man what he is after, and even Des can't ignore it any longer.

"I don't do penetration," Des says shortly, cutting off his touches with a gruff tone.

Paul half-recoils in the bed, as if stung. He had obviously thought he was onto something. Maybe it has just been a waste of a night. He makes some kind of half-articulate groan in the back of his throat, expressing disappointment and frustration.

The reaction is strong enough that Des does not reach over to pull him back, or suggest that they enjoy themselves in other ways. He simply lets Paul move away, watching him roll onto his back and close his eyes.

Paul falls asleep, disappointed, but drunk enough to slip away all the same.

Paul wakes up; Des pretends to be asleep and watches him through half-lidded eyes in the dark, making out only the outline of his shape in the dark. He is clutching his throat and gasping. He scrambles out of the bunk bed and onto the floor, and his footsteps pad heavily over to the bathroom.

Every moment that he is in there, Des wonders what he is doing and what he is thinking. He wonders whether his breath will even out now, or whether it will remain as raspy as it has been for the last ten minutes or more. He wonders if Paul realises what it means that he has to struggle to breathe. He wonders if Paul will say anything, or leave, or try to get his own back.

After a while, the toilet flushes and Paul comes back. It is only a matter of moments before he starts to gently snore. Des closes his eyes fully again, and drifts off to sleep himself.

He is woken by Paul climbing over him to go to the bathroom again, and sighs. The clock says 6am. So much for a nice lie in after a heavy night.

Paul wanders back in from the bathroom a few minutes later, looking more than a little disorientated. He has heavy rings of bruising around his neck, visible the moment he walks into the room, and as he walks closer Des sees that his eyes are bloodshot. In short, he looks like a man who has been strangled almost to the point of death in his sleep.

"You look awful," Des says, with the air of one who knows.

"Thanks very much," Paul replies sarcastically, partly out of a defensive reaction to his confusion.

"What happened?" Des presses, feigning sleepiness, staring at the bruising.

Paul shrugs; he does not know. In truth, he was probably hoping that Des would shed some light on it. That's certainly the last thing that he is willing to do.

"You should go to a doctor," Des says authoritatively. The act of care, he thinks, will remove suspicion.

He all but pushes Paul out of the door, fully dressed again in last night's clothes and with the dark marks on his neck obvious to the world.

Des lets him go and wonders idly if this will be the one that comes back to get him. He knows that he must have strangled Paul in the night; he doesn't remember it well, but then, his dear friend Bacardi was probably to blame for that. The marks in the shape of his fingers tell the story for him.

They will also tell the story for the doctors and nurses who look at him. This, indeed, could be the one that bites him. He knows he should probably have finished the job rather than letting Paul go, but once the chance was missed, it felt like it would be wrong to try again.

He waits for the police, but nothing comes. No one ever comes for him. He almost wants to laugh out loud with how ridiculous it all is.

Perhaps Cranley Gardens is a salve for him after all: something made him stop in the night, leaving a warm body rather than a cold one in the morning. What it was, he cannot say.

Chapter Thirty-Three

"Des, isn't it?"

Des looks around, startled to hear someone calling his name. He is sitting at the bar in the Salisbury Pub on St Martin's Lane; fair enough, it is one of his usual haunts. Perhaps not so unusual for someone to recognise him here.

He sees the other man and it takes a moment for it to click. Then it does, and Des remembers. "John!" he exclaims, nodding and laughing. He reaches out to catch the hand flung towards him for an excitable shake.

John had last been in Soho a few months back, perhaps in December, when they had met at a bar the first time. The tall, strong man had chatted with him for a few hours before taking his leave. They hadn't gone home together that time; Des had idly wondered if the other man would have liked to.

Perhaps tonight, he will find out.

"I'm just down from High Wycombe for the day," John explained as he waited for the barman to pour him a pint.

"Lucky meeting, then," Des replies. He isn't sure yet whether it is, but at least it's nice every now and then to have a friendly face to drink with. He finds it flattering that someone should deliberately seek him out a second time.

They had discovered plenty in common last time they spoke; Des remembers that John used to be a Grenadier Guardsman. With his own military background to expound upon at length, they make a good match, conversationally. Des doesn't mind telling stories about his time in Berlin, in Cyprus, in Aden. Not when he's got someone who understands.

They talk on at length, until John grows visibly irritated at the length of time the barman takes in coming back to pour him another pint.

"Service is shite in here," he moans. "Fancy finding somewhere else to drink?"

Des shrugs. "Fine," he says. He doesn't mind much. One pub is much the same as another in this area.

They head outside, and John casts a glance up and down the street. It's obvious, even without looking, that just about any pub will be as busy as that one was at this time of night. Des could have told him that, but on the other hand, he feels like seeing where this night will go.

"What about going to the offie?" John suggests. "Your place is near here, right?"

Des nods, and agrees. Why not? Get some Bacardi from the offie, head back home, cook some dinner – after all, it sounds like a pretty normal night to him.

They head back to the flat and eat dinner together while watching TV. John seems to have an opinion about everything they watch, but he starts to quieten down as the night goes on.

The late film comes on, and John yawns loudly. "I'm dead tired," he says. "D'you mind if I get some rest?"

Des does mind; he minds very much indeed. Reluctantly he inclines his head, not willing to go so far as a verbal assent.

John shuffles out to the bedroom, and Des tries to focus on his Bacardi and the film. He feels his blood boiling, seething just below the surface, but he tries to ignore it. It's just a friend taking a little rest in his home, after all. No real harm done. He would have offered the same to many of his acquaintances. For some reason, though, the easy manner in which John seemed to claim ownership of the right to do whatever he likes in Des' home really irks him.

When it comes past midnight and the film is over, Des wants to get some rest himself. John hasn't come back yet. Unenthusiastically, Des walks into the bedroom. He was hoping that John would have had the decency to come back through on his own. Instead, he finds him half-naked under the covers, as if totally at home.

"I thought you were getting your head down, I didn't know you were moving in," Des scowls, waking the sleeping man with his words.

John wakes up only a little, stirring slightly, and looking at Des as if he was rude to disturb him.

"It's late," Des continues. "Tube's off. Why don't I call you a taxi?"

John grunts, a guttural sound that doesn't exactly signify either yes or no. Then he closes his eyes and quite obviously goes back to sleep. For him, it seems, the conversation is over.

Des walks away for a moment and pours himself another drink. He is thinking it over. He doesn't like John anymore. He finds him rude and a poor houseguest. He doesn't find him attractive at all; has no desire for him to stay forever. In fact, he considers him an inconvenience, one which he would like to get rid of as soon as possible. He had hoped this could be done the normal way, through simply asking it. It seems that John won't be budged.

That settles it.

Under the cushion of the armchair, Des remembers he has left a length of loose upholstery strap. Perhaps it was the kind of thing he should have thrown away, but Des kept it instead, and hid it. He does not wish to consider the implications of why he did that; he snatches it up in a hurry, rushing to get the job done as quickly as he can.

He goes back to John and wraps the strap around his neck, as tightly as possible.

"It's about time you went," he says, climbing on top of him and pulling the strap tighter still.

John wakes again and struggles wildly; Des feels as though he is riding a bull, tossing and turning in an attempt to throw him off. John even manages to raise himself up partially and gets his own hands around Des' neck, and Des pulls tighter, trying to push him back down at the same time. For a short panicked while he believes that John will fight him off, or even strangle him first. From that moment it becomes a fight for his own survival, not just to get rid of John. Now he is battling to save himself. He won't be killed, not in this way, not in his own home.

Des summons some inner strength reserved from his army days and pushes John down forcefully enough that it actually works. His head hits the headboard with a dull thump, but he continues to struggle hard, and it is all that Des can do to stay on top of him. They are both half-out of the bed by the time he goes limp, and Des is panting for breath, and shaking.

There is blood on the bedding in front of him, where John's head bounced on the way down. He lets go of the strap and gets down onto the floor, watching John cautiously.

There is no sign of life, and dimly he realises that Bleep is barking furiously in the other room. She must have sensed the commotion; if she doesn't quiet down, the other tenants might start to wonder about what is happening upstairs.

Des goes through and kneels to Bleep, patting her on the head and fussing, shushing her. She quiets down at the reassurance from her master. She is always so trusting. She knows that he can handle whatever it is he says he can handle, even if he is shaking so hard that he can barely tell whether her tail is wagging or he is making her little body move. He is satisfied that she will remain quiet, and he can return to the task at hand.

Back in the other room, there is another shock. John is breathing again, though still unconscious.

Acting quickly, Des snatches up the strap and wraps it tightly around his neck again, and holds it there for three minutes. He waits out the time in his head, trying to find a way to calm his own heartrate down. He can't tell whether he is counting the seconds too fast or too slow against the rapid flittering of his pulse. This will surely be the end of it, now.

John's breathing seems to have stopped, and Des settles back onto his haunches, resting. He waits there for a few moments, catching his own breath again and trying to calm down.

Then, another surprise. Almost disbelieving what his own eyes are telling him, Des realises that there is still a little air moving in and out of John's body. He holds a hand to the bruised neck and finds a heartbeat, still going strongly as if nothing at all had happened. It even feels steadier than his own.

He cannot believe it, but if it is true, he has to do something. He falls back on that old resort, the one that has worked for him so many times in the past. He drags John to the bathroom and puts the plug in the bath. With John's head dangling right down as far as he can push it, he turns the cold tap on as far as it will go.

It takes barely a minute for the water to reach the level of John's nose. Des hears that raspy breathing come back again, as if the body senses imminent danger and is fighting for every last shred of oxygen. The water rises more, and John starts to struggle again.

Des isn't taking any chances this time. He holds him under for five, six, seven minutes. The water rises and rises, and John gradually stops struggling. Blood mingles with the water, first from the cut on his head and then from his mouth. Some other substance, a bile maybe, floats out of his mouth along with the last of the bubbles, and small particles of food.

Des lets go and leaves him there, turning the tap off but not draining the water. He isn't going to take any risks with this one. If he ever wakes up again, let him wake up to a lungful of water. That will teach him to mind his manners and remember that he is only a guest.

Tired and shaking, Des strips the bed and lays out a new blanket, too exhausted to consider putting out proper bedding. He lights a cigarette and feels the soothing touch of nicotine flowing through his system from the first drag, though it is nowhere near enough.

"Bleep?" he calls out, and the dog pads through, looking sheepish as if she has done something wrong. "Come up here."

He pats the bed next to him as encouragement and she jumps up, curling up against him. That is the warm and soothing presence that he needs. Over time, the combination of dog and smoke allows him to stop shaking. He finishes his cigarette, and at last goes to sleep.

It takes him three days to solve the dilemma of what to do with a body when there is no garden to be used.

Piece by piece seems to be the best way to get rid of it. No other thing for it, really: he can't walk out the front door with it, there's nowhere but the flat to store it, and he doesn't have the same kind of underfloor storage that he is used to. It will need to be reduced into smaller parts if he is to have any chance of removing it.

He covers the floor with bin liners just in case and then hauls the body out of the wardrobe and into the bath.

After a bit of thought, he lays a wooden board across the bath instead and the drapes the body over it. This makes it easier to cut off the soft bits of flesh into small pieces, around a couple of inches long. It gives him a flatter surface to work with, something to really lean on while he cuts and saws at the flesh. It is hard work, leaving sweat beading on his skin, and he has to pause often to rest his arms and hands.

Once they are cut off, the smallest pieces can be flushed individually down the toilet, like so much human waste. They have to be small enough that he does not risk clogging the toilet. So long as he manages that, they go down easily.

Des cuts pieces off for a while, but it takes a long time. He begins to grow impatient. In the old flat, he could have been bagging the limbs by now, almost finished. Here, he is restrained by the capabilities of the plumbing system, which leaves him limited indeed.

He hits on an idea, and starts putting bits of flesh and viscera and the skull into the pot to boil. This softens it all up considerably, and when he flushes the toilet with a bowl full of boiled flesh, it all goes down much better and in larger quantities. Even the brains flush down when the head is soft enough, scooped out with a spoon and a heavy heaping of irony. The chef's tools, put to work.

His knives come out to play, too, working on human meat again instead of steaks and hams. He starts breaking the bones apart, but his knives keep breaking. Such a frustrating process. Maybe he should have kept that set of chef's knives from that one near the beginning; they might have come in handy here. He could have been breaking someone else's knives rather than his own, at the very least, and professional knives tend to be stronger. He feels a little smart of shame that he, army chef Des Nilsen, doesn't have a good knife set to his own name just ten years later.

Finally, when the work is at last done at the end of a long day, he puts the bones into bin liners with a good dose of salt and places them in the wardrobe, along with some padding. As for the smaller bones, well, everyone knows he has a dog. He leaves them out for the dustman as if they come from some innocently slaughtered animal. No one will ever know the difference.

Chapter Thirty-Four

In the end, it all starts with the fantasy becoming real. He should have known that there was no way for him to really find a normal balance with his sexuality. Whatever it is that is inside him has been messed up, sullied and broken, and it will probably stay that way forever.

He is 27 years old the first time he has full sex with another male. 27 years of fantasy building up to that moment.

The memory is still as real and fresh as the day it happened. A special day, to be savoured forever.

He drops in to the gay centre, a little hall that is often filled with young, gay men in need of help and advice. He often wonders whether he is looking for help and advice himself, or just an easy mark. Whichever the case may be, he ends up finding one.

This night, there happens to be a young Scottish boy attending the hall. It offers warm drinks too, and that might be part of the reason why he snuck in. It has always been easier for Des to connect with Scottish boys – they warm better to one of their own. All the better when met in a place that doesn't require them to hide their sexuality.

They get on well through their little chats; after a while, there seems to be an unspoken mutual acceptance that the two of them will talk for as long as they can without the interruption of anyone else. It is an intimate feeling, a thrill that runs through the veins, the pleasure of being heard. So, they go out for a drink after the session finishes, and they start to get drunk, and fairly soon Des realises the boy has nowhere to go. No wonder he was so quick to accept the charity of a few free rounds from his new friend. No wonder he seems keen for the night to go on well into the early hours, wherever they can find a place to go.

Des proposes that he pay for a room in a cheap hotel so that the youth can have a roof over his head for the night. The youth, of course, agrees. Why would he turn down that charity for a damp cardboard box in an alley when it is offered by a friendly face?

On the way there, Des makes a stop to buy some more rum. There is always a need for more rum. One can't be expected to stay in a hotel room without a few drinks to extend the evening.

The youth drinks his fill and passes out on the bed, so drunk he can't even stay conscious anymore. He lays there prone, and Des looks at him, thinking hard.

For the first time, Des has an opportunity. He has a passive body and no one around to stop him, or even to witness it happening. He has the chance to make his fantasies cross over into the real world.

He pulls down the boy's trousers first of all. He needs to have him exposed. Then he picks him up in his arms and holds him for a moment.

It is everything he has imagined in his fantasies, alone with the mirror. A real, warm body hanging in his arms, limp and helpless. The boy does not stir or move; it is only the slow breathing in his chest that signifies he is alive at all. He is vulnerable in his nudity, and in turn that lends more and more power to Des. He feels like a god standing there.

He lays the boy down on the bed again and pushes into him from behind, thrusting until climax, and finally finishing his first full gay sexual experience. He has lost his virginity as a gay man. They always say that your first time should be special; this one certainly was. It was the collision between imagination and life. It was everything he imagined, and more.

In the morning, the boy does not seem to realise that anything has happened. For Des, everything has changed. It is a thrilling memory that he will cling tightly to for years to come; the moment when he saw that the fantasy could be real.

That the reality could be even better than the fantasy.

After that, there is never again a way to untangle reality from fantasy, never again a way to put his secret desires back into the darkness or hold them back any longer. The world of the mirror and the world that he lives in have become one and the same. The line in the sand has been washed away.

Chapter Thirty-Five

Des, as always, manages to astonish even himself by the way he is able to put it all out of his head. Surely, that is it now. Surely, there will be no more. It was so difficult to dispose of John, and so gruesome. Surely, he won't make the same mistake again.

He walks through the drizzle of a wet May afternoon to the Black Cap, a pub in Camden which he rather enjoys. It is bustling inside, though there are still a few seats available. He orders a pint at the bar and sips it when it comes, glancing around to decide what to do with himself.

Time and again, his eyes are drawn to a youth sitting on his own, nursing a half-pint, looking sorry for himself. He looks like he needs company even more than Des does. With a smirk of self-deprecation at that thought, he picks up his pint and wanders over.

"Mind?" he asks, one hand on the back of the chair facing the youth, hesitating just for the moment until permission is given.

"No, go ahead," the youth says, gesturing to the chair and scratching the back of his head. He seems almost startled, as if he was deep in thought and Des had woken him up.

"I'm Des," he says, never one to feel shy about initiating a conversation.

"Carl," the youth replies, giving him a small smile in response to his efforts.

"You look a bit down, Carl," Des says, taking a sip of his pint and smacking his lips. "Thought you looked like you needed a friendly face."

Carl shrugs at first, but can't stop the slow smile that gathers across his mouth. Des has hit home, it seems. "Thanks," he manages. He seems a little shy; a slight blush collects alongside the smile for a moment.

Des notices he hasn't really addressed what is making him feel down, but won't press it for now. The time for that will come later, after they have bonded a little. "Weather's shite, eh?" he says, nodding his head to the windows. A fine, misty rain is spraying down against them.

"Yeah," Carl says, and gives a half-laugh. "You've got that right."

"I mean, I can't complain," Des says. "In Scotland we call this a fine summer's day."

He gets a proper laugh now, and smiles in return. It was a cheap joke, but if it provided a way in, so be it. Even though most people wouldn't credit him with it, he is aware that not everyone appreciates a full diatribe on the plight of the worker during a first meeting.

They talk on a little while, at first about nothing, and then later about something. As he makes his way down another glass, Carl starts to loosen up a bit.

"I've just been feeling vulnerable," he says, sighing dramatically. It suits his youth. "My ex, well, it wasn't good. He would get so... angry."

"Violent," Des says, nodding. He can see it written in Carl's face already, before he opens his mouth. He doesn't need to be a mind-reader. The lad has carpet burns sprayed vividly down one cheek.

"Right," Carl says, reaching up to touch one of his eyebrows, as if touching the memory of a heavy bruise, and then the burns.

"Don't worry," Des smiles gently. "You're still pretty."

Carl seems pleased with that, although he soon lapses into the darkness again. "I stayed with him for far too long."

"You could have done something," Des says, and in his mind's eye, he sees a replayed memory of himself throwing something across the room at Twinkle. He pushes the memory out of his head and looks at Carl innocently, taking a sip of his pint in case there is a ghost flashing across his face to hide. He might have a bit of a temper, but he's never been bad enough to hurt a boy like that.

"I was too scared to go to the police," Carl says, sadly. "I mean, not because of him, even. Because of them. I only turned 21 last month. If I'd have gone to them, they would have been on at me about being too young for gay sex and it would have turned into something different. I just wanted him not to hit me, that's all."

Des nods sympathetically. "Can't trust the police," he agrees, even as he acknowledges inwardly the truth that he would have been in prison long ago if they had ever taken any of those who ran from him seriously. "They've got their priorities all in the wrong order."

"I was worried about a lot of stuff," Carl continues, shaking his head. "Thought it was all my fault, sometimes."

Des reaches out impulsively and touches his arm at the wrist, just where it bends to meet his beer glass. "It wasn't," he says, imbuing a knowing confidence into his voice. "It's never the victim's fault. Violent men like that will always be violent, no matter what you do. You could be perfect, and he'd still have been violent."

Carl looks up at him and smiles gratefully, his eyes shimmering wetly. "It's good to hear that," he says.

Des leans back in his chair again, satisfied that he has made the right impression. It's not that he wants to manipulate him, exactly; just that he knows he has more chance of company tonight if he gets Carl eating out of his hand.

Their talk turns to other things as they finish their drinks, and soon their glasses are empty. Seizing on the opportunity, Des stretches and nods towards the door.

"Fancy going somewhere the drinks don't cost an arm and a leg?" he asks.

"What, leave London?" Carl jokes, grinning.

Des laughs. "No, just leave the pub. We can head back to mine, pick up some bottles on the way, if you'd like."

Carl smiles again, and nods, almost springing to his feet. "Let's go," he says, enthusiastically.

They get a cab together, and impulsively, Des reaches out and takes hold of Carl's hand. In the secrecy of the back seat, he doesn't pull away. They smile at one another like schoolgirls.

The taxi driver doesn't seem to know where he is going; Des glances out of the window and realises they are taking the long route home, and he can't believe the man is trying to dupe them.

"Hey," he says, angrily. "You're taking the long way 'round."

"This is the quickest route," the driver says lazily, not even glancing in his mirror.

"No, it's not," Des scoffs. "You can't fool me, pal. I live here, right? You're trying to get us to pay a higher fare."

The taxi driver steadfastly ignores him and drives on. Des is seething; he can't stand people who try to pull that kind of game. He says nothing else. They are at the mercy of this man, after all, who could easily lock them in the cab and call his mates to beat up the two poofs he has picked up. Des sees those images in his mind and keeps quiet. He isn't being a coward. He's a realist.

As they get out of the car, Des sorts through his pockets and counts out the fare in the smallest change he has. The petty act gives him a little thrill. He may not have managed to change the situation, or punish the man really, but it's a little bit of gratification at least. Now he can get on with the better part of the night.

Back at the flat, though, things don't go quite as he hoped. A couple of drinks down and Carl quickly manifests as the dreaded sad drunk. He moans on about his ex-boyfriend, the opportunities he has missed in his short life, and even about his first boyfriend, who apparently was so kind and wonderful and nice. Even though he mentions that Des reminds him of that boyfriend, the compliment is not enough to offset the complaining.

Des is tired, and tired of it. He moves a little closer to Carl and leans in to kiss him. Happily, Carl kisses back, and soon they are cuddled up tightly and making a real go of it. Bliss: quiet between them, only tender and loving embrace, hungry kisses teasing the possibility of something more when they have worked up to it.

That's until Carl breaks away to be sick.

It's obvious that the Bacardi has been too much for him, and when Des exasperatedly suggests that they just go to sleep, Carl makes no argument. They get into bed together, but neither one of them so much as tries to initiate anything beyond a little casual fondling.

"Watch out for this," Des says gently, indicating the jagged zip which has broken away from the edge of his sleeping bag. He is using it instead of a blanket lately. "It's loose. You don't want to get it wrapped around your neck."

Carl looks around at it, and nods. "I'll be careful," he says, snuggling himself up closely against Des again.

Des is only a little sure that he means it as a genuine warning. Part of him wonders if it would be interesting to see Carl tangled up in it in the middle of the night after all. That part of him waits, coiled like a tiger ready to pounce, while Carl falls asleep in the darkness.

Laying there, in the dark, Des thinks about everything Carl has told him. About how he is a victim, and maybe destined to always be a victim. His trusting nature, and the way that he simply walked to the flat after Des showed a sympathetic ear, point to that being a strong likelihood.

He thinks about everything Carl has been through, and how sad he is now. How lonely and miserable. How it takes only a drink or two to unlock all of that sadness and pour it out onto the world.

Really, it might even be a mercy to him. Such a sweet, young lad would never stick around with an older man like Des; it would just be Twinkle all over again. Maybe if he stays forever, in that other way, it will be better for him, all told. Des will be able to look after him. He will be able to make sure that nothing, and no one, can ever harm him again.

When he has finished thinking about it, Des finds himself with a tie wrapped around Carl's neck. He hoists him up so that he can pull it tight from behind, and holds it even when Carl wakes and starts to struggle.

"Keep still," he says, and although Carl only stops struggling for a moment, he is weak enough that it makes no difference. It takes only another minute for his body to fall limp, and Des lets go of the tie.

He puts it back where it came from, over the back of the chair, and turns to deal with the body. That's when it surprises him. Carl takes a shallow breath, his chest rising and falling, and his eyelids flutter momentarily before he falls back unconscious again.

Des watches him in wonder, almost stupefied for a moment. Another? Is he losing his touch? It's ridiculous how many of them wake up after being strangled so tightly. Anyone would think that this was Des' first time. He won't waste any more time on this one with the tie. Straight to the bathroom, that's the only way: he has learned that, now.

He pulls Carl to the bathroom, noticing how his eyelids flutter open and closed every now and then. He is drifting in and out of the world, perhaps aware of the pain in his neck and his lungs. Regrettable, but it will all be over for him soon. The suffering will only be short-lived.

He runs the taps and drapes Carl across the bottom of the bath, positioning his head right next to where the water hits the white surface so that his nose and mouth will be covered quicker. As the water begins to build up he struggles weakly again, nothing that Des can't handle.

He feels the fight ebbing out of Carl, bit by bit. He feels the moment when he gives up. "Please, no more," Carl manages to gasp out, half into the water. It sprays and burbles out of his mouth with every word. "Please, stop."

Des closes his eyes and holds him firmly under the tap.

After another minute he figures that enough is enough. There's no need to torture the poor lad's body any further, leaving it lying in the cold water. This one is not ugly like the last, and he wants to keep it special if he can, keep it pure. This is not a punishment, but a gift.

He takes it and lays it back on the bed, his routine a little disrupted by the change in method; he decides that he will wash it – and himself – later.

Perhaps in the morning, when he has sobered up. Then perhaps they can watch a film or two together.

Bleep runs into the room, and, strangely, right to the bed. Normally, when there is a dead body in the room, she simply ignores it. He has never seen her go up to one before, not even for an idle sniff, since he warned her off the first time.

He is just about to call out her name and drag her back when she does the oddest thing: she starts to lick the body's face.

"Hey, weed," Des says, finding his voice again after a moment of hesitation. "Come away. Come here, that's it."

Bleep looks at him and whines, and back at the body again, before running to his side. She is far too loyal to disobey him, but there is an obvious reluctance in her delay. Des gets up, with Bleep wagging her tail at his feet, and walks over to him.

Then he sees the eyelids fluttering again, and nearly jumps out of his skin in fright.

He's still alive. Carl is still alive. Des thinks of his sweetness, his earnestness, his trusting nature. His warmth and his desire to be loved. He springs into action and grabs blankets from the wardrobe, wrapping Carl in them as tightly as he can. He starts rubbing Carl's body all over, trying desperately to get him warm again.

"Come on, Carl," he says, pausing only to turn the electric heater up on all bars. "Come back to me."

He keeps going, rubbing and holding him, trying to impart as much of his own body heat as possible, until he starts to see clearer signs of life. Carl stirs a little but does not open his eyes, and his breathing becomes steadier. Checking his pulse, Des finds that it is running closer to a normal speed. His skin is warmer now, too, not cold and clammy as it was before.

Des steps back, breathing hard. He's done it. He's saved him.

Now he just has to hope Carl won't remember why he needed saving in the first place.

Chapter Thirty-Six

Carl sleeps for so long that Des begins to think he was wrong, that he didn't save him after all. But he is still breathing, and every now and then he will shift or groan in his sleep. Des takes that as reassurance enough, and waits for him to wake properly.

When he does, a full day has already passed. Des eyes him nervously as he gets out of the bed, a red mark vivid and obvious against the skin of his neck.

"What...?" Carl murmurs weakly, leaving the sentence hanging in the air unfinished, as he gazes at his neck in the bathroom mirror. A hand hovers somewhere near his collarbone, as if afraid to touch the marks.

"I did warn you about that sleeping bag," Des says. "You got all caught up in the zipper."

Carl frowns. Did he warn him? Was this really done by a zipper? He looks closer at his reflection. "I was caught?" he asks, trying to understand.

"Yes," Des repeats, hoping sheer force will help Carl to accept it as the truth. "I had to wrestle you out of it. It was wrapped around your neck so tightly I thought you would die. Then you slept for a long time. I've been monitoring your breathing. Honestly, I was afraid you were going to die right there in my bed."

Carl cocks his head slightly, then winces. Des can almost see the cogs turning in his brain. There is a flicker of something, some kind of suspicion, replaced almost immediately by doubt and then an odd kind of certainty.

"You saved me, then," Carl says. "I'll have to be more careful from now on."

Des could almost weep with relief. He has no idea how he managed to convince Carl that it was the truth, but somehow it has worked. The lad must have been desperate enough to believe that there was an innocent explanation that he fell for it, totally and completely.

"You should go to a hospital," Des suggests. "Check there isn't any lasting damage."

"Right," Carl agrees, and gathers his things. It's clear he doesn't want to wait, just as it is clear that Des won't be accompanying him, however genuine his concern may be.

"I hope we'll meet again," Des says as he walks him down the stairs and to the door of the flat. Part of him really, earnestly means it. The lad was good company, and there is a delicacy to him that needs to be protected. He should have someone around him who is willing to look after him. Des feels a flutter low in his stomach at the thought of being that protector, one day.

"I'm sure we will," Carl says as he turns to go, but the lad is too honest. Des can read in all the lines of his face and his body that every word was a lie.

Chapter Thirty-Seven

Does saving Carl make him a better person? A changed man?

Though he wants to believe it desperately, part of him knows that it is unlikely to be the case. Stopping himself from killing the others who escaped him didn't work. Being questioned by the police didn't work. Moving house didn't work. Perhaps there is one thing that would work, the possibility of a real life domestic bliss, but he doesn't believe that it is within his reach any more. Those dreams walked out of the door a long time ago.

There is one occasion that helps him to think that he might become a better man again, all the same. He takes Bleep for a walk to Highgate Woods so that she can romp around a little; he is watching her carefully as she runs ahead. When she starts sniffing around a blanket with a bulky shape, he approaches with caution.

"Bleep, leave that," he tells her, and she backs away uncertainly, growling quietly in her throat.

The blanket is wrapped around a very particular shape, now that he looks at it, and there are dark red stains which he recognises as recently-dried blood. Just looking at it makes him feel queasy. That is enough to have him backing off in horror, too.

He has stumbled across a dead body.

"Come on, weed," he says urgently, and Bleep runs to his heels as he walks swiftly back the way they had come. "We need to report this."

He is totally shocked by the sight, by the idea of a body out in the open like that. Anyone could have found it. Surely, any murderer that could leave a body like that is a real threat to public safety. No regard for the idea of getting caught – no regard for what innocent eyes may see!

As soon as he gets back to the payphone they had walked past, he places a call to the police, urgently informing them of what he had found.

He walks back to the blanket, so he can watch over it in case someone tries to retrieve it or cover it up before the police arrive. Then he waits, his heart racing and his palms damp, for them to come screaming up the road in a car with red and blue lights. He has always feared that sight pulling up under his own window. Now he is anxiously awaiting them.

He wants to be instrumental in the capture of this man. He wants the papers to say that Des Nilsen, 36, of Muswell Hill, discovered a body in Highgate Woods whilst walking his dog. He wants them to catch the man before someone else gets hurt.

The police arrive in due course, though not quick enough for his liking; they have an active crime scene to investigate, after all. Still, they are courteous enough, and when he shows them the blanket, they go in for a closer look.

The righteousness Des is feeling turns to chagrin the moment they lift the corner of the blanket, and reveal a dead dog.

He should have known, perhaps. Bleep only sniffs around live humans, not dead ones. The police tell him that he did the right thing, but he can see past the veneer of customer service and read the annoyance plastered across their faces.

He doesn't blame them. How embarrassing – how stupid – to have called in a tip about a dead dog and got himself so worked up about a serial murderer stalking the parks of London. Now he feels like even more of a fool than ever.

Chapter Thirty-Eight

He is walking by Piccadilly station when he spots a tall and rugged man trying to hail a cab. Not likely to be any luck for you at this time of night, Des thinks derisively, not in that state. The man is definitely the worse for wear, probably high, judging by his eyes. Des only realises that he has been staring at him for too long when he is close enough to see that there is blood on his jacket.

Strangely, that neither worries nor excites him. It is just one more detail to notice.

The man is aggressive by nature, it seems, shouting something to Des about looking at him. He has a broad Glaswegian accent, and Des grins.

"Nice to see a fellow countryman," he replies, and something in the other man's nature relaxes.

"Nice for you, mebbe," the Glaswegian retorts. "None of these lot seem to want to see me at all."

He gestures to the passing taxis, and Des laughs. "They're busy this time of night," he explains. "You'll be waiting a while, honestly, unless you call one for yourself."

"Fat chance of that," the Glaswegian replies, finally letting his arm drop and turning his attention away from the road. "You know where I can get one, then? I'm dying of hunger. Thought I could get a cab to a mate's and see about getting a meal."

Des looks at him for a moment; his rugged looks, his tall and thin frame. He can't be 30 yet. Despite the obvious signs of addiction, there is something appealing about him. "I could see about putting something together for you, if you want," he suggests.

"Yeah?" the Glaswegian asks, rubbing a grimy finger against one of his temples.

"I don't know if I've got much supply in, but it'll save you getting a cab at least."

The Glaswegian changes immediately, his demeanour rounding out, a smile appearing on his face. "That's great," he says, slinging an arm around Des to slap him on the opposite shoulder. "What a great chance to bump into you, eh?"

Des revels in his role as saviour as they journey back to Cranley Gardens, allowing his new friend to go on at length about his gratitude. When he calls himself Puggy, though, Des has to laugh.

"Puggy?" he asks. "What's your real name, then?"

He expects something ridiculous, but Puggy laughs back and taps the side of his nose. "Not Puggy, I can tell you that. A lot more boring than Puggy."

When they get back, Des discovers that there really is, as he had thought, very little supply in. On the plus side, he does have a whole tray of eggs, so an omelette seems destined by fate.

He makes the omelette and serves it up, not feeling too hungry himself, and settles in front of the television with a good old Bacardi and coke.

At length, he looks up, and realises that Puggy is no longer moving. Three-quarters of the omelette is gone, but the rest remains on his plate; indeed, one small piece is even hanging out of his mouth. Des stares at him for a minute, trying to think back. He didn't hear any choking, nor did he notice any unusual movements in his peripheral vision. Could his guest have choked on the omelette even despite these facts?

He pours himself a new drink and works his way through it, thinking. It won't do to have a police investigation sniffing around his flat, should Puggy have expired. As always, it seems, he has left himself in a tricky situation by not clearing up his messes quickly enough. There's certainly no time to get rid of a whole body from his wardrobe before an ambulance can get here. Which means he can't have them coming here, not under any circumstances. It's not a floorboard situation anymore. Things are more serious here.

If Puggy wakes up and moves, that will take the situation out of his hands, but Puggy does not so much as stir. After a while, Des wonders what there is left for him to possibly do.

He finishes the drink and then stands up, and walks over to the other chair. He takes the plate and the rest of the omelette and puts it on the coffee table, safely out of the way, and then returns to Puggy again.

A while later he looks up from his armchair and sees red finger-shaped marks on Puggy's neck, and knows without having to check that he is no longer breathing. There is a large gap in his memory from right around the time he put the plate down.

He tries to tell himself that Puggy has expired due to an unfortunate choking accident, but an omelette cannot put its hands around a man's throat. He supposes, in the end, that it must have been him.

Chapter Thirty-Nine

An old favourite image: The Raft of the Medusa by Gericault. There is an old man half-kneeling on the raft, his head supported on his hand. With the other hand, he holds in place the exposed and pure body of a naked, dead young man. The old man's arm and knee contort the body's spine in such a way that he is displayed all the more openly, as if the old man knows that Des is watching and wants him to be able to see the best bits. He pays no mind to the other men on the raft. This boy is his sole focus.

He replays this image over and over again in his mind, and brings it to life. He imagines the old man reaching down to the water that surrounds and furiously buffets the raft, and using his own hands to sluice water over the dead body to wash it clean. He imagines him laying it down on the raft then, amidst all of the other dead and dying men, and having his pleasure. Sending the body off with a true fond farewell.

To bring a little variety into the fantasy, Des moves to the next figure in the painting. A muscular black man is waiting just at the old man's elbow, seemingly undressing a body of his own. Des likes to imagine him with the same splayed body, or with another young man of a similar sort.

Sometimes the black man comes into his own; steps right out of the painting and into the modern day. Des pictures him holding aloft and carrying the dead body of an emaciated young junkie, overdosed and gone. The more emaciated the youngster, the more powerful and muscular the black man becomes in his mind.

Even the imagined scene of the one holding the other is sometimes enough. The eroticism of it, the imbalance of power, the play between death and life, is so intense that it will never leave his mind. It is burned onto the backs of his retinas, onto his very soul, if he has such a thing. The line between his mind's eye and the things he really sees always seem so blurred. The one thing he is sure of is the pleasure of it, the delicious images that run through his mind, from the mirror to the painting to his own imagination.

Chapter Forty

If there is one spark of brightness in his days, it has to be the fact that work seems to be going so much better than before. Now that he has his promotion at last, and he is working in a much more nurturing environment, it feels like he has made real strides forward. Perhaps one day, he can even take Janet's position – though he would always hope it would be because she was promoted, herself.

He loves to throw himself into the work. He even starts to take home little things he can do outside of working hours, like drawing graphs and charts. He takes pains to ensure that every little detail on them is right. These are important documents, after all, and can't be completed in any old haphazard way. They must be done to a professional standard.

He understands why the others at work don't want to take it on. It's very careful work, not the kind of thing you can do if you're going home to kids screaming and the nagging of a wife. He has the time and the inclination, and he takes pride in the fact that he can get it done. It's one more thing he can contribute to the office.

Des gets a letter from his mother before the year is up; as Christmas approaches, it starts to play on his mind.

Dear Dennis, it reads. *Well, you'll be another year older on the 23rd and I still don't know how you are getting on. It will be seven years come Christmas since you have been home. I have been enjoying myself more lately now that all of you children are grown and left home, but I still want to know about your lives. I wonder if you are thinking about getting married soon?*

It's true that they have not spoken properly in such a long time, but he does not want to go home. He does not want to let her know how he is doing. So typical of his mother: not even a Happy Birthday, simply a moan about her old lonely self and how miserable it is that she has not seen him. So selfish.

But something happens that makes him think again, if only for a moment. She calls him that December and they talk on the telephone, for the first time in a long time.

He is still processing it when he goes in to work; seeing that Janet is alone in her office, he wanders over for a chat.

"I had a call from my mother," he says, introducing the subject with a modicum of unusual shyness.

"Oh, that must have been lovely," Janet smiles. She knows that he does not communicate often with his mother, and he wonders briefly if she meant the comment as a joke.

"Hardly," he scoffs. "Well, I've not much time for her diseased old ramblings. Honestly, it's a wonder the woman doesn't get the message. All us brothers and sisters left the nest and spread out from her, and she doesn't think for a minute that maybe she's the reason we wanted to go."

Janet seems to brush his statement off; she has a good relationship with her parents, and so Des supposes she can't really get what it's like. "What did she want to talk about?" she asks.

"Oh, just the usual rubbish," Des tells her. "What am I doing, how's work, am I married yet, you know? Pestering on at me with mundane loquacity. Talk for talk's sake."

"It's nice to connect with family," Janet says, her tone halfway between a suggestion and a statement.

"Aye, your family, mebbe," Des retorts. "She went on at me about this marriage business. As if a man's happiness and a mother's success can be measured by how quickly and how well he marries. The woman just never manages to catch on."

"You still haven't told her about your... preferences?" Janet asks, the smallest of pauses while she works her way around to a PC word to use.

"She wouldn't listen even if I told her," Des says, rolling her eyes. "Half an hour we talked for nearly, and I barely got a word in edgeways. All Olav this and Sylvia that. I don't know why she thinks I want to know how my siblings are getting on. I haven't seen *them* for just as long as I want to, thank you very much, and I haven't any care as to what they do with their lives."

"You don't get on with your brothers and sisters either, then?" Janet asks.

"Oh, no, never," Des shakes his head emphatically. "Last thing I heard from Olav was how much he hates poofs. Of course, mother never caught on to that reference either. She was still blathering on about my age and how I have to think about starting a family sooner or later. I don't know why she goes on so much."

Janet smiles smoothly, patting his arm. "She's just trying to show that she cares, Des," she reassures him.

Des talks on and on until they both have to get back to work. He can't believe she called him. Most of all, he can't believe his traitor heart, which warmed and swelled with joy that someone would take so much of an interest in his life with every question that his mother had asked. Perhaps if he focuses on how much he dislikes the old woman, he'll be able to convince himself that it's all really true.

When Martin comes to visit again, just for a few days as always, Des feels a surge of hope added to the lighter feeling in his heart. It seems like everyone wants to pay him a bit of attention these days.

"Des, what is it about that smell?" Martin asks, looking around the living room at Cranley Gardens. "It seems to follow you around."

"What smell?" Des retorts. He likes to think that he takes very good care of his own personal hygiene; his time in the army saw to that.

"That mustiness," Martin says, sniffing the air. "You had it at your old place, too."

Des sniffs the air a little. It worries him. He has become so used to the smell of the dead bodies in his house that he has almost forgotten it is there.

As soon as Martin is gone again, Des goes out and buys a new stack of deodorant sticks. He lays them out carefully, hoping that at least this will make the smell a little less noticeable again. Can't have people getting suspicious, after all.

The thing to do would be to get rid of them completely. But, like disinfecting the bath or auditing his wardrobe for worn-out and ill-fitting clothes, it is an unpleasant chore that he can never quite remember to get around to. Even when he does, those few and fleeting attempts make little difference considering the scale of the task at hand.

One day soon, he will have to apply himself: get as drunk as possible and get rid of them completely. But that day is not today, nor is it tomorrow. It is some distant place in the future that he does not yet have to think about seriously.

Chapter Forty-One

On the 22nd December, Des heads out to Soho – very much as per normal. It's a busy night, but he still manages to catch the eye of a likely young thing, a car thief just on his way back from serving time in Belgium. What an odd combination for a man to be, Des thinks, listening to his story and running an eye over his 20-year-old body whenever he thinks he won't be caught. The prison sentence doesn't worry him, nor does the theft, though on some level he knows that it should. What could anyone steal from a man who has already had everything destroyed once?

Trevor, his name is, and he has decided to stop over in London before heading home to the Midlands. They share a few drinks together, and Des suggests that he comes back to his flat. He positions the offer so that Trevor will think about the idea of staying for a few days, saving money on a hotel. He wants him to stay.

He accepts, and heads back to the flat with Des readily. Des is in high spirits. How wonderful, to have a friend to share the Christmas season with. It's a rare chance that has him feeling the festive spirit at all.

"Why don't you sleep in one of the armchairs?" Des asks, pointing to the comfier of the pair in the front room, when the two of them have had enough to drink. He isn't gay, and Des knows that the offer of a bunk together in the one bed he has available would be refused. If there were any slim chance, he would have made the offer. Trevor has a lot going for him, even if he does have a poor record.

"Oh, thanks," Trevor replies with a brief grin, settling himself in with a little shimmy of his shoulders.

Des goes to bed in his own bedroom, leaving him to it. He wonders dimly what he will find in the morning: a body, a burgled flat, a bunch of car thieves having a conference about some big job. He tosses and turns in his sleep, but never has the compulsion to go through and check. The morning will hold what the morning holds.

In the morning, as it turns out, Trevor is still there. A turn-up for the books, at least.

"Why don't you stay a few days?" Des offers as he serves up breakfast. It's an offer that makes sense, and they both know it. Now that Trevor is settled in, it is almost a formality only: they both understand that he will stay until it is more convenient for him to travel on.

"Thanks, that would be great," Trevor agrees gratefully. The deal is done.

"I've a couple of days of work during the week," Des tells him. "But you're welcome to have the run of the place. It'll save you a bit of money at least, eh? And you won't have to be on the streets at this time of year."

"Yeah, I really appreciate it," Trevor grins. "It's a bit awkward going home at this time of year anyway, you know? No one's happy with me for getting put away."

"Don't worry about it," Des replies. "There's no judgement here, hn?"

When they have finished eating, Des leans back and stretches out.

"It's days like this," he says, starting up what he can feel inside will be a long talk. "When I think about the plight of the worker. The government don't do us justice. We should have more mandated holidays, so that everyone can get some fair time off. D'ye know how many extra men they always want us to lay on for catering at this time of the year?"

Trevor shakes his head slowly and hesitantly. He doesn't seem to realise that it was more of a rhetorical question.

"Marx had it right," Des says, the beginning of one of his favourite proletariat speeches, and he does not drop the subject for the rest of the day.

He remembers at some point after dinner, with a few good doses of Bacardi inside him, that Marx is buried in Highgate Cemetery. It isn't too far away, but no amount of coaxing can seemingly persuade Trevor to come and visit with him. Ah, well. The boy's own loss. Des resolves that he will go on his own sometime soon, and bow down before the great master of communism.

Trevor seems happy enough, although they do not celebrate anything together in any real way. On Christmas Eve and even on Christmas Day, there is no special occasion. No big meal, no friends or family coming to visit, no presents, no fuss about the time of year. Just the two of them and Bleep, and a steady flow of rum and coke.

On Boxing Day, Des cooks a stew. He mistimes it, getting distracted by his own hunger, and pulls it off the stove before it is really cooked to satisfaction. The potatoes chunks, in particular, are still quite hard, and the meat is a little on the dubious side.

"This isn't cooked very well," Trevor blurts out, staring at a piece of meat on his fork.

Des stops eating and stares at him. "I did my best," he says, a little snappily.

"It's disgusting," Trevor says, pushing a piece of potato around in the broth with his spoon. "We'd be better off feeding this to the dog."

Des gets back to eating without saying a word. He is fuming inside. He prepares this boy a free meal – no, *six days* of free meals – and that is the response he gets? His anger does not subside as he stubbornly eats the whole bowl, pretending not to watch Trevor leaving his own portion on the floor for Bleep. Ungrateful little scrote. He should have kicked him out into the street on Christmas Day, see how he liked begging in the cold for scraps instead of getting everything handed to him on a plate.

Des pours himself drink after drink, half to soothe his fury and half to mask the taste of the stew, which in truth wasn't even good enough for Bleep. He notices morosely that she has only eaten half of the bowl that was offered to her.

It is getting late, and as it passes midnight, Des is most of the way through his bottle of Bacardi. He feels as though layers are being stripped away from him, both by the anger and by the drink. Each layer allows him to move a little closer to the surface. Each one allows him to speak his mind a little more.

"I'll have to consult with the professor to see if you can stay," he mutters threateningly to Trevor. He barely knows what he means by it himself, except that it sounds menacing, and the idea of having another person inside of him ready to dole out justice is an appealing defence for his conscience. Despite his exhortations, there is no sign of shame or apology on Trevor's face.

The other man gets up and mutters that he is going to bed, and Des sits alone and rages.

It does not take too long for him to decide what he is going to do. He first considers bashing him over the head with something blunt and heavy, but he has a pretty face; it won't do to ruin it. Then he looks over into the kitchen and sees his trusty kitchen knives and imagines stabbing him, but it is not something he finds very tasteful. He doesn't want to risk the blood, certainly not in the kind of quantities that stabbing would cause. That option is out, too.

What about tying his legs together and strangling him? Strangely, when he thinks about it like that, Des finds that he can't bring himself to do it. There's something about the act that always happens spontaneously, in a way. To plan it out this rationally and in advance makes him feel very strange about it. He opts not to go down that route.

What is next, then? Another old favourite remains. If he uses fire and smoke to asphyxiate him, well, that will be a fine idea indeed. No need for a physical attack; no need to even be in the room. Just set it up and let him expire, and come in the next morning to take care of what remains. It sounds perfect. In fact, it will even leave his body more pure and clean, without the ugly red marks that always appear on the necks. In many ways, it is perfect.

He grabs a pair of jeans at random and wets parts of them so that they will cause flares of smoke. He puts them in the living room, and uses a cigarette to deliberately light them on fire.

He lingers a little to look at the fire and ensure it catches, and then a moment longer to take in Trevor's sleeping form, curled up on the chair.

Then he goes into the kitchen and pours himself a glass of water. He will enjoy a cool and refreshing drink, and perhaps clear a little of the fog out of his head, before going back to stop the fire getting out of control.

To his disappointment, Trevor rushes in before long.

"The room's full of smoke," he coughs, holding the front of his shirt over his mouth. There is a frantic look in his eyes.

"Is it?" Des asks, far too casually; he mentally kicks himself into gear. He needs to at least pretend to be concerned.

"Something's on fire," Trevor says, more urgently, throwing open doors and windows within reach to help the smoke clear a little.

When Trevor discovers the smouldering jeans and points them out to Des, he shrugs his shoulders.

"Oh dear," Des says. "I must have dropped a cigarette on them. How silly of me."

Trevor does not challenge him; at least, not verbally. There is a look in his eyes that says he knows Des for a liar, and sees a danger in pointing that out.

In the morning, he says that it is time for him to move on.

"You must come stay again, next time you're in town," Des says cordially as he sees him off at the door. He means it, too.

Trevor doesn't even glance back as he heads off up the road towards the station.

Chapter Forty-Two

Des has been drinking all day, every day since Trevor left. It is now New Year's Eve; the last moment to enjoy 1982. He figures he might as well see it in with his favourite activities. Drink, a good film, and a walk with Bleep in the afternoon to keep her happy.

But as the day wears on, he begins more and more to get the feeling that this is not the kind of day that should be spent alone. It's a moment that requires acknowledgement: the passage of one year into the next. If you don't celebrate it, if you don't mark it with people around you, then your life might as well be one long monotone.

He has had more than a few Bacardis already, but the swaying of the walls doesn't stop him from stumbling downstairs to knock on the door of the two young women. Vivique and Monie- no, no, that's not right – *Monique* and *Vivienne*, their names are.

With that fact firmly grasped in his head, he listens through the door as they both come towards it, then open it, leaving him nearly swaying right through into their home.

"Ah," he says, steadying himself. "I wondered if I might invite you two delightful young ladies upstairs to watch some television."

"Television?" one of them repeats. They exchange a glance with one another.

"There's lots on," he says, raising one arm in an upwards gesture, towards the vague direction of his television set. "New Year's stuff. Great fun to watch. Thought we could all keep each other company on the big night."

"Oh," one of them says, and they look at one another again, slowly beginning to shake their heads.

"Sorry, Des, we've just started cooking dinner," the other one says, raising her shoulders in a defensive shrugging gesture.

"We thought we'd make something special," says the first one, her face all upturned like it has melted all of a sudden, making a mask of sorrow that surely must be exaggerated. "It's going to take a couple of hours to make, I'm afraid."

Rude bitches. They're obviously making up an excuse to avoid spending time with him. The looks they give each other show that they can think of nothing worse than spending the New Year with Des from upstairs. Des wants to shake his fist right in their faces and tell them he's far too good for their company, anyhow.

But in the end, he is still lonely, and he does very much want their company. "Well," he says, straightening himself up haughtily. He does not have the sobriety in him to try to hide the disgust in his tone. "I'm going for a drink at a pub around here later. If you can bother to shift yourselves from the stove for that, you are invited to join me."

He turns on his heel and walks back upstairs, never giving their door a backwards glance. That's the last time he invites either of those two foreigners out anywhere, and that's a fact.

He gives up waiting anxiously for them to come upstairs and leaves at around 11. He throws a foul glance at their door as he passes, lifting up two fingers in a rude gesture when he is sure that they are not watching him. He can go and have as much fun as he likes without having to rely on people in this flat, and that's a fact.

With only an hour to go until the countdown, the pubs around are already packed. Everyone is in a celebratory mood, cheering and laughing together, drinks practically flying through the air.

It's not too hard to find another young man standing on his own at the bar. With everyone clustered into big, friendly groups, the ones who are still alone are easy to spot.

He's Japanese; one of Des' favourite types, with his smooth, boyish body and young looks. Finding an Asian man in London is not as common as he would like it to be, and even rarer still for that Asian man to be gay. Des can't resist going in for a pry, to see what he can find out about this stranger.

The man certainly looks relieved to be approached. He's probably too shy to try introducing himself to someone else in case he accidentally offends or breaks the rules of his adopted culture. His English isn't too bad, though, not too bad at all.

"Toshimitsu," he says, after Des introduces himself. Des buys them both a pint, as custom dictates, which they raise towards the ceiling as the countdown comes.

Everyone chants together, loudly as possible, like demented, drunken cultists. *Ten, nine, eight, seven, six, five, four, three, two, one – Happy New Year!*

There is cheering, whooping, and plenty of kissing in the pub after that. Everyone around them is caught up in the heady joy of it, and both Des and Toshimitsu can't help but grin along with them. What a fantastic night. What a feeling of being alive.

With the countdown done, though, there doesn't seem much point in sticking around. The party starts to dissolve, breaking down into smaller groups, and the atmosphere is one of departure.

"D'ye fancy heading back to my flat?" Des asks, bending forward to shout into Toshimitsu's ear over the din. "I've got Bacardi, some other stuff. Cheaper than here. What d'ye think?"

Toshimitsu looks up and simply gives him a grin and a nod, and the two of them drain their glasses and head out of the pub.

Des can barely remember getting home, but suddenly there they are, swaying dangerously up the stairs into his flat. They are giggling under their breaths as they go, more out of a shared delirium than any joke or amusement. It's the New Year; no need for a reason to be cheerful.

Their camaraderie can only last for so long. This night, of all nights, feels like a fateful night to Des. It calls back to that first time, that first lonely New Year's Eve when he decided not to be lonely anymore.

He is trapped into a cycle now, and he must continue it at all costs. If he leaves them alive, they will leave. Anyone you meet in a pub is bound to leave, sooner or later. That's the nature of London's flighty and fleeting pub scene. If he wants them to stay, they have to become bodies. But when they are dead, he must rid himself of them eventually. He can't enjoy their company forever.

So, he must add to them.

He grabs a tie with both hands, and stretches it out between them, like a garotte. He doesn't care that Toshimitsu is not asleep or unconscious this time. It doesn't matter that he is probably sober enough to fight back. Des is ready to do it, right now, and that is all that matters.

Toshimitsu pushes him away roughly, laughing at him. "What is this?" he splutters, almost spilling his drink. He seems to think it is all a big joke. Maybe it is, to him.

Des tightens his grip on the tie and goes for him again, lunging forward to get it around his neck. This time, Toshimitsu is no longer laughing. He pushes him for a second time and yells, something wordless, or something Japanese perhaps.

Des takes it harder this time; stumbles back and into the coffee table, which instantly tips over with him. He finds himself on the floor amongst a clatter of bottles and glasses and ashtrays. Bleep bounds through from the other room, barking, unsure whether to go to her master's side or try to warn off the stranger.

"What are you doing?" Toshimitsu shouts angrily. He is standing over Des now, glowering, panting hard.

"What'd you push me for?" Des shouts back, trying to get a grip on his tongue for long enough to make the words come out right. "Me coffee table…"

"You're crazy!" Toshimitsu yells, backing off and going to pick up his coat from the back of the armchair.

By the time he has it in his hands, Des is on his feet again, and wielding the tie with a vengeance. "Don't call me crazy," he growls, jumping towards him again. "I'm gonna get rid of you."

They start to brawl, hitting the floor early on and rolling, banging heavily into bits of furniture as they go. Toshimitsu appears to have sobered up quickly, as if he realises that he is truly fighting for his life.

As they roll, Toshimitsu finally manages to get the upper hand. He manages to get a knee into Des' groin, leaving him writhing on the floor. Toshimitsu rushes to his feet and out of the door, leaving his jacket behind. Des grabs a torch off the side and runs after him, but the other man just has enough distance ahead of him to stay in front. They both rush down the stairs, a headlong race for the front door.

Toshimitsu trips and falls right at the end, hitting the ground rather than the last few steps, and Des hears a desperate sob erupt from his chest. Then he reaches the front door and is through it, slamming it behind him.

Even though he picked up the torch so that he could chase him, something inside Des tells him that now, enough is enough. Toshimitsu is gone. There is no way he will be able to catch him now, and if he runs out into the street after him, there will only be more of a scene.

The door to the flat near the foot of the stairs opens, and Monique and Vivienne peer out. Des turns his torch off, but it is too late; they have seen him already, in the light that spills from inside their front hallway.

"Are you alright, Des?" one of them asks, quietly.

He nods at first, catching his breath. "Just…" he begins, trying to think of a good enough lie. "Just a bit of a misunderstanding, that's all."

He leans against the wall, unable to stand straight without support. The whole corridor is spinning now, not just the walls, and he knows that everything he tries to say is coming out slurred. The Bacardi and the pints are catching up with him rapidly. He wants to vomit.

"Alright," one of them says, not entirely sounding convinced, and they both retreat back inside the safety of their own flat.

Des waits a moment until he hears the door lock click into place, then heads back upstairs slowly, to sleep off the booze.

Chapter Forty-Three

Des is just on his way home when he gets into a conversation with a Scottish youth who is hanging around on the roads, even though the evening is approaching. He is very young – perhaps around 20 or so – and does not look in the best of health. There is a wild look in his eyes, and Des feels somehow drawn to him. He looks like a lost lamb in need of a shepherd to guide him.

"I'll walk to the tube with you, if you like," he offers. "I was going to stop for a hamburger on the way."

"I haven't eaten all day," the youth, who mentions his name is Stephen, tells him. Looking at him, Des believes it.

"Then come with me," Des says, clapping a hand on his shoulder. "I'll get something for us both."

They walk to the McDonald's on Oxford Street and wait in line. Stephen is noticeably jumpy, and his pupils are dilated. Des knows a drug addict when he sees one. Whatever he might be on, he's on it right now, and it is far from his first time. Des keeps his mouth shut; there are decisions a man may make in his life, and it is not for anyone else to try to change them.

After the food, they go to the off-license. Des buys a couple of bottles of Bacardi for himself, and six cans of lager for Stephen. They are both in good spirits, Stephen even more so for the free food and drink, and Des even more so for seeing the effect they have.

Somewhere along the way, they have decided that Stephen will come home with him to eat and drink; they won't part ways at the station as they had planned. It happened almost organically, though Des suspects that Stephen was hunting for a bed in the first place. With this change in mind, Stephen hesitates outside the station.

"Will you wait for me, just for a few minutes?" he asks, making a pleading face. "I've got to just tell my friends over at Centrepoint that I'm not going to meet with them."

"Alright," Des agrees, glancing around at the half-empty streets. The evening is setting in, and it is freezing cold. "Just don't be too long."

He stands alone, scuffing his boots on the ground, leaning against the wall. He appreciates the irony that for the moment, he probably looks as much of a drifter as his young friend does. He sees his breath steaming in the air, and watches openly as people hurry past, studiously avoiding his gaze. London is a bit like that. Everyone looking at the ground instead of at each other. Perhaps that's why he can't seem to resist getting into conversation with these street urchins, who are as desperate for attention as he is.

Just as Des is checking his watch and thinking about leaving, Stephen appears out of the gloom, striding down the road with his hands huddled in his pockets and his breath streaming white behind him. With a nod and a quick greeting they are off again, and just after 9pm they make it back to the flat in Cranley Gardens at last.

They eat; they drink; they are merry. At one point Stephen slips off to the toilet, for far too long compared to the amount of time he should need. Des guesses he must be injecting himself with something. You don't get that kind of look in your eyes from taking nothing. He must be so hooked that he can't go a single night without a hit.

There are scars and bandages on his wrists, too, glimpsed when he reaches his arms out and his sleeves rise up a little. Des says nothing – not his business, really – but they bother him, like an itch he can't scratch. All of it bothers him. Stephen shouldn't be injecting himself, or cutting himself, or sleeping on the streets. No one should go through that, and no one should put themselves through that, no matter what their background may be.

When Stephen gets back from the toilet, whatever he took makes him sleepy. He dozes off in the comfortable armchair with the television on, so Des decides to entertain himself. He puts on his stereo headphones and listens to *Tommy* by The Who.

He sits on the carpet and drinks his way through one of the bottles, lost in his own world of music. With the headphones on, everything else goes away; it seems coloured differently, somehow. As if the themes, the ideas, and the emotion in the music become imbued in everything around him. He has always felt a little bit like he is in a film when he listens to music, the backing track that the audience will hear as his scenes play out.

He gazes steadily at Stephen's sleeping form, pathetic and limp, scrawny and in obvious need of help. His tight black jeans that reveal how skinny he is; the thick jersey that won't be enough against the winter cold; the leather jacket meant to make him look tough; the blue and white football scarf, a flash of colour, perhaps a flash of something real.

The music changes; now it's *Theme from Harry's Game* by Clannad. There's a quality to the music he can't explain. The ethereal sounds, the Gaelic tongue, the sorrow heavy over the whole track. It settles deep into the nooks and crannies of his soul and makes him feel it in every particle of his body.

Finally, he finishes the last of the glass. The music has finished. He takes the headphones off and gets up, knowing even as he does so what it means. What he is going to do. He looks at Stephen again, crashed out completely on the combined effects of the drinks and the drugs.

He walks over and kneels down in front of Stephen, almost in a position of obeisance, and touches his leg. His own heart quickens in anticipation. "Are you awake?" he asks.

There is no answer. Stephen lies still and prone.

Oh, Stephen, Des thinks. *Here I go again.*

Casually and slowly, as if looking for another glass or a bite to eat, Des goes into the kitchen and finds some thick string he knew was in the drawer. Then he lays it out on the draining board and looks at it; it's clear that it is not long enough.

The cupboard in the front room yields an old tie that he no longer has any use for. He cuts a bit off it, attaches it to the string, and throws the rest away. He has a fine ligature now, a fine tool.

He goes back into the room and finds Stephen still sleeping. Bleep follows him in, tail wagging, interested to see what her master is up to.

"Leave me just now, Bleep," he says, giving her an affectionate scratch on the head. "Get your head down, everything's alright."

She wags her tail once more and heads off into the front room, probably looking for a soft and warm place to curl up until he calls her again. Des wonders if he is protecting her, sending her away. She knows what is going to happen. Or she will know, once she senses the life gone out of the body that was here alive only a while ago.

Des remembers some half-wisdom learned somewhere that the *thuggi* in India would knot the string for a quicker kill, so he tries this for himself. Then he takes the ligature and puts it over Stephen's knee, hesitating for the moment.

Another drink will help. He pours it, feeling his heart beating so fast it can barely be contained within his chest.

He sits on the bed for a moment and drinks the Bacardi, looking at Stephen again.

All that potential, all that beauty, and all that pain that is his life, he thinks to himself. *I have to stop him. It will soon be over.*

Des does not feel like an evil man, or even like he is doing something bad. This boy needs help, a release. He cannot be doing something wrong if he is freeing Stephen from pain.

He gently takes the scarf from around Stephen's neck and sets it aside. He picks up one of the youth's hands and lets it go; it flops back into place, boneless. He pulls open one of Stephen's eyes; there is no reaction. Stephen is so deeply asleep that he will likely never feel a thing.

Des kneels by the side of the chair, facing the wall, and drapes the ligature around Stephen's neck. Then he takes each loose end of it and pulls, hard.

Stephen's arms and legs feebly raise into the air, the hands as if reaching for Des' own neck. There is a small and weak struggle that barely lasts a minute before his limbs drop down again, limp. He has weakened himself with the drugs and the drink, until his body can no longer put up any kind of fight at all. Des holds on for a couple more minutes just in case, then releases him.

Stephen is no longer breathing.

"Stephen, that didn't hurt at all, did it?" Des says, soothingly. "Nothing can touch you now."

Des runs his fingers gently through Stephen's bleached blond hair and pushes it back from his peaceful face. He is gone now. It is done.

The body is wet with urine; Des wonders if he might have defecated too, and knows that the body must be washed.

He first takes a drink and a cigarette; they will help to calm his nerves, stop his shaking. Once his heart comes back to something resembling a normal speed, he can get to work.

The body has not made a sound. It is soiled and must be washed, so Des runs a bath at a hand-warm temperature and adds in some lemon scented washing-up liquid.

He strips the body; the jeans are so tight, and wet now, that it takes him some trouble to get them off. At last, with Stephen sitting naked in the armchair, he can see that he has only urinated. Probably, he supposes, because he has not had a square meal in a while – not until the hamburger, which will still be in his system.

Des notes that he has ginger pubic hair, but nothing over the rest of his body. Smooth and hairless, just how he likes it. There are crepe bandages on Stephen's forearms, which Des removes to find deep razor cuts. They are still open, still fresh. It looks as though he had tried to commit suicide recently. Very recently.

Des casts an eye over his face again. He has got his wish now. He is gone to the better place.

Des picks up the body and carries it in his arms to the bathroom, where he places it into the bath and washes it carefully. He ensures that every part of the body is clean and purified, even turning him over to wash his back.

When he is satisfied, he pulls the slippery body out of the bath and sits it on the loo to dry it off, getting his hair as dry as can be possible with only the use of a towel. Then he carries it over his shoulder into the other room, where he places it on a chair for a moment.

Its eyes are not quite closed, he notices.

Stephen, he thinks, *You're another problem for me. What am I going to do with you? I've run out of room.*

He can't fit any more bones in the house, and the flushing method takes time. But he won't think about that now. He won't ruin the moment.

He lays the body down on the double bed and arranges the mirror so that he can see it, then strips himself off and lays down next to it.

Staring at them both in the mirror, he notes that the body is paler than his own. Well, he is ginger, after all: it is to be expected. Des gets out some talcum powder and puts it on himself to make them the same, then lays down next to it again.

"We look so similar now, Stephen," he says out loud, watching the pair of them together. "Look how beautiful you are. Look how beautiful I am."

He lays there watching them both, simply staring. He does not move or react; that would ruin the tableau. Two dead bodies, laying next to one another on the bed, exposed and limp.

"You're so lucky to be out of it all now," he says to Stephen, smiling as he admires him. "You're so sexy now. So fabulous. Look at you, hn?"

He stares and stares, and that is enough. He doesn't even get aroused. He just wants to look at the pair of them, like this, forever.

Eventually he begins to feel tired, and cold. Laying still and naked for so long has taken its toll. He gets in between the sheets, leaving the body lying on top next to him. He does not bring the body under the sheets; he knows that soon it will be getting very cold, and he does not want that lying against his own skin.

Bleep wanders into the room with her tail wagging, perhaps sensing that whatever has been going on is over at last.

"Come on, old girl, get your head down," Des says, smiling at her eagerness as she jumps on top of the covers. "Stephen is all right now. He's okay."

Bleep settles down at the end of the bed, pausing only once to sniff Stephen's leg and then ignoring him completely. She is wise. She always knows the difference between a person and a body.

Watching her curl up, Des feels sleepy too. He turns the head towards him so that he can kiss it on the forehead. "Goodnight, Stephen," he says, and switches off the light without waiting for a reply.

A few hours later, he wakes up. Time to get ready for work.

The body is cold, as predicted, so he carries him into the front room and lays it on the floor. He straightens the body out so that it will not set into a strange position during rigor mortis, and then covers it with a blanket.

After that, he gets ready for work and goes out. It's a normal day ahead. Finding men for jobs; finding jobs for men. He is his usual cheerful self, with no hint of what might have happened the night before.

Chapter Forty-Four

On the 3rd of February, there is some kind of commotion going on in the rest of the house; Des at first does not notice it.

After work, he is coming into the house when Fiona from downstairs stops him. She always talks too much. From her rambling conversation Des understands that her parents are coming to visit, and that Jim will not be in the house with her while they are around; hence, perhaps, the reason for her anxiety over some kind of issue with the toilet.

"So, is yours blocked?" she concludes, having barely drawn breath.

Des frowns. "No, mine's fine," he tells her. "No trouble."

"Right, well, just watch out for anything with the plumbing," Fiona says. "We've had to stop using these down here for tonight. When you flush the other one, it makes the water rise in ours. And ours isn't going down at all, so we're risking a flood if we use them at all."

"Will do," Des says, nodding. He simply wants to get away from her. He walks up the stairs, hoping she won't shout something after him; she doesn't. He doesn't care much about what those two rude bitches downstairs have to deal with, and Jim and Fiona have never been particular friends. Let them sort out their own troubles.

Up in his own flat, with the door closed, he knows that he has work to get on with. Stephen isn't getting any fresher, and it is time for him to go away – permanently.

He has had such fun with him over the last week. He has discovered a new play: picking up the body and letting it limply drop onto cushions on the bed, it holds a new fascination for him. This is something he has not tried before, and he is pleased to have discovered it now. Still, there is no more drooping to be done for Stephen. He is past that point now.

Des gets out a black bin bag from the kitchen and cuts the side of it, so that it will lay open like a sheet. This done, he lays the body carefully onto it, as carefully as if he were trying not to hurt an injured comrade. He must show respect to this body, which has given him so much pleasure.

He takes his sharpest knife and cuts off the head. This time, there is rather more blood than he expected, somehow. Perhaps something scientific to do with the drugs in his system at the time of his death. Anyway, he doesn't know about all that, but what he does know is that blood is spilling off the sheet and onto the carpet.

He quickly grabs another black bag and lays it out in the same way. As he passes, he puts the head into a pot of boiling water on the stove, and turns on a second burner so that it will heat quicker.

He reverently moves the body over onto the second black bin liner, taking care not to spill any more blood in the clean-up operation. Then he carefully picks up the second sheet and takes it through to the bathroom.

He curses as more blood spills out from the overloaded sheet onto the white carpet of the bathroom floor. Why did it have to be there, the most obvious place in the house? Once the sheet is disposed of, he grabs some paper towels and starts trying to mop it up.

It's no use; the stain is obvious. There is no way he can get it out of the carpet now.

Des remembers that he has some pieces of brown carpet in the wardrobe, unwanted and left over, so he takes one and places it over the stain. Perhaps it looks a little odd, a randomly placed section, but it will do the job of covering it up.

He grabs Bleep's lead and calls her over, resolving to finish the rest later. There's no rush. While he is bringing Bleep back from her walk, he swings by the Shepherd's supermarket to grab a few things. Cigarettes, Bacardi, Coca-Cola. The essentials.

That night, he watches television and listens to classical music through his headphones, enjoying the sounds of an orchestra. He drinks three-quarters of the bottle of rum that he had picked up, and then turns off the gas. No need to leave the head cooking overnight; he lets it lie in the pan, though, ready for another go at it tomorrow.

He goes off to sleep, Bleep curled up in a ball of warmth at his feet.

Des doesn't wake up again until 11am the next morning. Some way to sleep off a late night and a hangover! There's some noise going on outside, but he dismisses it. Probably just the people from downstairs trying to sort out their toilet problem. Des is just glad that his still works.

He doesn't bother going outside for the whole day; it's Saturday, and he can do what he wants. What he wants happens to be watching television and relaxing, so that's what he does.

At some point in the mid-afternoon, there is a knock at the door.

Des freezes and turns the television down quickly. He cannot answer the knock; if it is someone that he knows, he will be in trouble. How can he explain to them that they can't come in? He glances across the doorway to the other room, to the headless body lying on the floor. No one can come in right now.

He picks up Bleep and holds her tight, so she will not go and bark at the door.

At last, he hears steps walking away, down the corridor and back down the stairs. He relaxes and breathes deeply, only realising then that he had been holding his breath as much as possible.

That was a close one; he can't let that happen again. He should have cleaned up earlier and not left it all to chance.

Later, he prepares to go out with Bleep for her evening walk. He notices something fluttering on his door as he opens it to step through: a note, left for him to read.

Plumber has been don't flush the loo

Des pulls the note from the door and tosses it inside. So much for his working too, then.

As he is reaching the bottom of the stairs, Fiona emerges from her doorway, and he groans inwardly.

"Did you see the note?" she asks, pointing upstairs as if at his door.

"Yes, I did," Des replies, hoping she will leave it at that.

"We had the plumber come out this morning," she continues, oblivious. "He had a look under the inspection cover and inside the toilets and everything, but he couldn't find it. The blockage, I mean. So, Jim had to go and call Dyno-Rod but, you know, Ellis have to approve the work."

Des nods. Ellis & Co are their agents. If they're going to be paying for the expensive plumbing visit, they need to have it all signed off in written paperwork first. "Can they do that on a weekend?" he asks, in spite of himself.

"No, we've got to wait 'til Monday," Fiona says, shaking her head and rolling her eyes. "Can you believe it? Anyway, until then, Mike says – that's the plumber – he says we're not to flush any of the toilets. I know, I know, it's annoying. I want it fixed as soon as possible but we have to wait."

"Aye," Des says, nodding in sympathy. Then he gestures to Bleep, as if suddenly remembering that she is there. "Well, I'd better get this one off for her walk."

Bleep gives a little yap at the word 'walk', as if on cue. Fiona laughs and waves them off.

Des walks away, letting Bleep run on ahead out of the house and onto the street. Inwardly, his mind is turning. A blockage in the toilets; one that can't be cleared by normal means. Is it coincidence that he has been using the toilet for means that aren't exactly what it was intended for? A deep vein of worry flashes through his head. He had better hope the two issues aren't related. If they are, this might be it for him.

He goes home after Bleep has had her fill of exercise, and sits to watch television. He doesn't go out that Saturday night. Can't, anyway, not without a place he can bring anyone back to.

Chapter Forty-Five

Monday, he thinks, is likely to bring up some very awkward questions. Sunday, then, should be spent preparing for them, if at all possible.

He gets on with cutting up the body. It has to be done. If there is going to be a knock on his door from someone with the authority to enter, he would really prefer that it did not come when he has a body on the floor and a head on the stove. Even if he has nowhere to hide them that isn't inside the flat.

Some parts of the body go into plastic bags in the cupboard. Some go into plastic bags which he places on the bathroom floor. He's running out of room, so he takes a drawer out of the chest and places it upside down over the bags to hide them.

The head goes last inside one of the cupboard bags, and then a few deodorant sticks go on top of everything. That should do the trick, at least for now.

He goes to work on Monday morning feeling the pressure. He is sure that there will be some kind of confrontation when he gets home. He is short and snappy all day, mostly at the expense of his colleagues.

"I'm sorry," he tells one of them, after a particularly explosive remark. "I'm just under great pressure at the moment."

The woman looks quizzical, but Des shakes his head and gets back to work.

When Dyno-Rod finally get to the house on Tuesday, it is after Des has arrived home from work. The tension and pressure for the last couple of days have been unrelenting. He almost hates the man simply for the fact that it has taken so long for him to show up.

At around 7pm, the other tenants seem to drift into one room in the house, and Des follows them. He has been listening and looking out of the windows as much as he can, trying to keep an eye on the proceedings.

"I'm just going to call my manager," the Dyno-Rod man, Michael, announces to the room. "He'll help get this sorted out."

Jim has a dark look on his face and Fiona looks worried; the others are just as puzzled as Des pretends to be. He has a feeling about what Michael is about to say, and it is leaving a pit the size of a fist in his stomach.

"Right," Michael says, looking very much like a man gearing up to say something he is going to have to explain in depth. "So, I lifted the manhole cover and had a little look down into the sewers. There's a smell coming out of there and I can tell you, from what I've seen of sewers, that's not how they're supposed to smell. Honestly, it reminded me more of rotten meat. Not only that, but I've had a look at the pipes and there's a lot of grey material coming out of them. It looks like flesh to me. We're going to have to have another look at this tomorrow in the daylight, but I have to admit I don't like what I saw."

Des listens to his explanation with the knot inside of him growing tighter and tighter. This is it. It was him. He's the one that blocked the toilet, and he's been doing it with bits of his bodies.

"No, there's no Indians in the house," Michael says, glancing around, apparently in response to some question from his manager. "Yeah, that sounds like a plan. Alright. Yep, I'll let them know."

Michael finishes off his conversation with his manager and puts the phone down; then he turns to the tenants and starts answering their questions. There is a lot to think about, apparently, with the most pressing concern being where the meat could have come from.

"You've got a dog, haven't you?" he asks suddenly, turning to Des. "Do you put dog meat down the toilet?"

"No," Des says reflexively, holding the mask tightly in place over his face and hoping that it will fit.

But there is something brewing inside of him. Some kind of idea that what he just said might turn out to be a lie. That maybe, he has been putting dog meat in there after all, or meat of some kind. Meat of any kind, so long as it doesn't come from a human body.

Jim suggests that they take a look at this rotting meat again, so he and Des and Michael head outside with the light of the torch bobbing around in front of them. They all lean down to look inside the whole in the ground, covering their noses at the smell and examining the flesh. Des pretends to make shocked noises as if he has never seen anything like it before.

Once Michael is gone, Des takes his leave and heads back upstairs. A plan is forming, and he needs to put it into action.

His first step is to go upstairs and write a letter to the agents. He complains at length about the unpleasant odours from the drains and how long it has been since the problem arose. He is thinking while he writes it that this could be something that removes him from suspicion. If he is making an official complaint and drawing attention to the problem, then he surely can't be responsible: only a fool would do that.

There is no risk of delaying too much by writing the letter; he has to wait until late at night for the rest of his plan anyway, when everyone else is in bed.

After midnight, Des steals out of the house and into the garden, carrying a torch and one of his trusty black bags. He removes the manhole cover, trying to place it down carefully, but it makes a little noise all the same. Then he climbs down the steps and starts scooping.

He picks up all of the flesh that he can find and scoops it into the bag. When he has removed everything that he can see in the light of the torch, he retraces his steps to the garden and throws the bag over the other side of the garden hedge.

When he walks into the house, Jim and Fiona stop him in the corridor.

"Where have you been?" Jim asks. There is something accusatory in his tone.

Des looks down at his torch, held in his hand, as if to show Jim that his question is stupid. It isn't stupid. In fact, he uses the opportunity to check there is nothing obviously incriminating on his hands and arms. "Just went out to have a pee," he says, innocently.

Jim backs off, but Des can feel him watching as he goes up the stairs.

It had been a brilliant plan. All he had to do was buy some chicken from KFC, cut it to the right size and soak it for a while, then go back down and throw it in the drains. Then in the morning, everyone would feel stupid, and he would sheepishly admit to being the culprit. He would be reprimanded for throwing dog food down the toilet, and that would be that.

But now, Jim and Fiona have seen him. Not only does he believe that they would know the truth, would be on alert to stop him if he went back to the manhole cover again, but he feels the weight of it all on his shoulders now, too.

What he has done, he wants to stop. If he carries this out and gets away with it, there would be nothing to stop him doing it again to more innocent boys. He would do it again, he knew, in his heart of hearts. He would kill again because it was easy, and nice, and took away irritations, and stopped people from leaving.

He is sickened by all of it. The things he has done in the past; the way he is acting now, the way he can't stop twisting things in his own favour. Playing games. Acting one way to conceal what is going on underneath.

He is sickened by the thought of the future. Any future. The guilt is a burden which he can hardly contain any longer. The weight of it drags him down like concrete.

He briefly flirts with the idea of suicide, like his Stephen. He drinks down a Bacardi and coke, and shakes his head. What would a man like him say in his note? How could he ever convince anyone that what he wrote was true if he was no longer around to tell the fantastical story in full detail? All that evidence gone – no way the police would find any traces of anything now unless he could lead them to it.

Doesn't he owe them that? The men, the families of the men? Shouldn't this incredible story be told to the whole world, so that they can be remembered? The people they have left behind deserve to know what has happened.

Bleep comes over and sits beside him, and he looks at her and knows that there is one big reason he cannot leave this world that way. If he killed himself, he would have to kill her first. It would be the only humane way. He could never do that, not to her. He could never look into her trusting eyes and watch the life drain from them the way he has with all of the others.

Running is not an option; he knows that, too. He isn't stupid. He knows that he would be caught.

Time to accept it, then. He gathers Bleep up and holds her tight, that last warm beacon in this world. Her lovely influence in his life has been something worth living for. He owes her one last night.

He holds her until he can no longer stay awake, luxuriating in that warmth and comfort, knowing it is likely the last time he will ever have it.

Chapter Forty-Six: The Man, Drowned

Michael isn't due back until later in the morning, so Des gets up and goes to work as normal. It is easier, now that he has accepted everything.

He dresses in his normal clothes: his dark trousers, his pale grey tweed jacket, his dark blue tie, his blue shirt, and his wire-rimmed spectacles. As a final flourish, a kind of homage to the day, he puts Stephen's blue and white football scarf around his neck.

He wonders idly about what kind of scene will face him when he arrives back in the evening. Since Dyno-Rod are coming to the house so early, he imagines the police will be there by the afternoon. After that, it won't take too long for them to figure out there is something serious going on.

Maybe they will go into his flat when he is not there, and be waiting for him with handcuffs.

Des tidies his desk as much as he can, and arranges it in such a way as he would want to leave it on his last day of work. Then he gets out a piece of notepaper, and writes a quick line: *If I am arrested, there will be no truth in any announcement that I have committed suicide in my cell.*

He puts the note into an envelope and half-hides it at the back of his desk. That will do, for now. A fragile kind of cocoon against any kind of injustice that he may end up facing.

He tries to act as normal as possible around his co-workers. He even manages to be quite cheerful, if such a thing can be believed. The weight of the world is almost off his shoulders now, and that knowledge is enough to lift the burden at least a little bit.

By the time the end of the day comes, he is feeling almost misty-eyed about his workplace. There have been ups and downs here, and surely he was deserving of much more than he ever received. But this has also been the job that allowed him to enjoy his union duties, and to get into politics in a much more effectual way. For that, he is grateful.

On the journey home, he worries incessantly, feeling the moment drawing nearer. What will happen to Bleep? What about the next of kin of his victims – how will they feel when they find out what has happened to their loved ones?

By the time he gets home, a little after 5.30pm, he is quite ready for whatever will come next. Still, it is hard not to fall back on old habits when he sees what surely must be a group of policemen outside the house.

"Hello," one of them says, as he approaches. "I'm Detective Chief Inspector Jay from Hornsey CID. I've come about your drains."

"Since when have police been interested in blocked drains?" Des asks, giving him a wry smile.

"I'll tell you more when we get inside," Jay replies. "If you would...?"

Des nods and leads them inside, giving a quick glance back to the two other men in plain clothes. "Health inspectors?" he asks, nodding in their direction.

"No," Jay says, sounding faintly amused. "Detectives."

They walk up the stairs, and into his flat. They are here, finally. Standing on what might as well be hallowed ground. They are here, and it is too late to do anything about them.

There is a smell in the house that Des has never quite been fully able to mask. It is a smell that is obvious to those who recognise it, and he knows that Jay will recognise it. He couldn't fail to.

"Your drains were blocked with human remains," Jay deadpans, his face completely straight. The two of them are playing a game together, now. Almost an enjoyable one.

"Oh my god, how awful!" Des deadpans back. The right words. The right reaction. But there is nothing genuine behind it, and it shows.

"Don't mess me about," Jay says. "Where's the rest of the body?"

Des takes in his expression, and knows what he needs to do. "In plastic bags in the other room," he says.

He points out the wardrobe, handing over his keys so that they will be able to open it.

"I won't open it for the moment. The smell tells me enough," Jay says, taking the keys. "Is there anything else?"

"It's a long story," Des says. "It goes back a long time. I'll tell you everything. I want to get it all off my chest. Not here, but at the police station."

Then it is all over. In a flurry, things happen all at once. He is arrested and read his rights. Jay takes him back outside to the car and they drive away from the house, another detective sitting beside him for the ride back.

"Are we talking one body here, or two?" the detective asks, out of the blue.

"Neither," says Des, with his characteristic flair. "It's sixteen."

There is an odd silence hanging in the car for a moment, as the detectives process what he has just told them. He glances around, and he can see they are taking him seriously. It is the magnitude that has struck them.

He allows himself a wry smile in the back of the car. It began with a Stephen; it ended with a Stephen. There is some kind of poetry in that.

Now, at last, they can put him away somewhere where he won't be able to do any of this ever again. Finally, he can stop.

Author's Note

This book has been, at times, difficult to write. My biggest difficulty and struggle was in hoping to do justice to the victims, not all of whom have been identified, whilst at the same time presenting the story through the eyes of their killer.

With that in mind, I wanted to honour their memories and who they were, and the people they left behind who grieved for them.

There are a number of other victims who are not mentioned here. Nilsen's official total is 15, though it is now thought that three of them may have been imaginary creations. Throughout his life in prison Nilsen has shown difficulty in separating imagination from reality, and now says that he made them up in order to live up to a tally he had created spuriously in the back of a police car. Some of the events in his life that relate to his fantasies prior to murder may also have been elaborated or invented.

In this book, you have read about 12 victims who died, as well as the ones who escaped. The disputed victims are identified as an Irish labourer; a hippy; and a skinhead with the words 'cut here' tattooed on his neck. Whether they existed or not is something we may never really know – the evidence of their deaths would have burned into ashes on Nilsen's last bonfire.

Stephen Holmes was 14 years old when he was allowed to attend a pop concert in Willesden. He was on his way home to Kilburn when he met Nilsen. Mrs Kathleen Holmes campaigned for information about Stephen's whereabouts until her death in 2002, at the age of 62. She never knew what happened to her son. His father, Francis, and sister, Deborah, only learned of his fate in 2006, when a missing person's file was identified as possibly being the 'Irish teenager' Nilsen had talked about. He was able to confirm it was Stephen by looking at his photograph.

Kenneth Ockenden was 23 years old. He had saved up for months to take a trip around his favourite childhood haunts, and to visit members of his family who had remained in the UK when he and his parents emigrated. He made regular calls home and to a relative living in London, who raised the alarm when he did not call on time. Just before he met Nilsen, he had spoken to his uncle about his plans for getting back to Canada before Christmas. After he did not show up again before Christmas, foul play was suspected; his parents flew to the UK to do a press conference in February, appealing for information. Nilsen watched their television appearances.

Three years on from his disappearance, they were still earnestly searching for him, with 'missing' posters going up around London. It was only a few months later that Nilsen admitted in a police interview room that Kenneth had been his second victim. He was formally identified through fingerprints on his A-Z London Street Guide, which Nilsen had kept.

Martyn Duffy was only 16 when he met Nilsen. He had been through a troubled time: dropping out of school, sleeping rough in London, taking drugs, and engaging in casual gay sex, he seemed to be living an aimless life. One psychiatrist he was seeing helped him to get onto a catering cause – the source of his chef's knives – and hold down a girlfriend. Despite all of this, he ended up back in London again in May 1980, where he met Nilsen at the station.

Nilsen accidentally kept hold of a few of the knives he had found at the station in Martyn's luggage, although most were thrown away. The ones that remained had Martyn's name on them, allowing police to formally identify him.

William, or Billy, Sutherland was a father of one who was also going through a turbulent time. Aged 25, he had enough of a rocky relationship with his girlfriend that she did not raise the alarm after he stopped calling home – Edinburgh - from London. After news of Nilsen's arrest hit the headlines, Donna realised with some shock that the timelines matched up. She called Billy's father, who in turn spoke to the police. Nilsen confirmed that Billy had died at his hands with a mere nod of the head after seeing his picture.

Malcolm Barlow had suffered from epilepsy at an early age, and was struck a serious blow at the age of 11 when his mother died. His sister Doreen tried to look after him, but he proved to be an unruly youth. He would lie, steal, sleep with men, and then blackmail them. He started claiming benefits and moved around often, which no doubt contributed to the difficulty in identifying him as a missing person at first. It took hard police work to discover that he was one of Nilsen's victims.

John Howlett was 28 years old and enjoyed a lifestyle of casual work, often helping out at travelling fairgrounds. He had left home as a teenager and the life seemed to suit him. The search for his identity was difficult as Nilsen knew him only as John the Guardsman; when it transpired that he had not, in fact, been in the army, it was almost impossible to identify him. Finally, the search was narrowed down when his blood type was taken from a strip of tissue. He was one of the hardest to identify of those whose names we know.

Graham Allen, known as Puggy to his friends, was 28 years old when he ran into Nilsen. He was a registered heroin addict and had a past as a petty criminal, but he was also boyfriend to Lesley and father to Shane. He was totally heterosexual, and would have had no interest in Nilsen as a romantic partner. He had been laid off by the steelworks at the age of 17 and so moved down to London to find his fortune.

After meeting Lesley he seemed to calm down for a while, but it was not to last. Young Shane saw his father drifting in and out of rehab and prison, never staying home for long. Graham argued with Lesley on the night he disappeared, yelling at her from outside as she refused to let him in. He punched himself in the face, high and drunk, until he bled from the mouth. Eventually Lesley shouted at him to, "Fuck off – and never come back!". To her shame and despair, he never did. He was able to be identified through dental records.

Stephen Sinclair was born Stephen Guild, but was adopted shortly after birth. He was known to welfare workers as incredibly volatile: on one occasion he threatened to pour a can of petrol over himself and light himself on fire. He was a drug-taker, thief, and tested positive for Hepatitis B. But he was also known as a good friend to many in the West End area, with a sensitive and friendly personality.

He was identified through a number of items: his football scarf, which Nilsen had openly worn to work; his leather jacket; and his syringes and tobacco tin, which retained his fingerprints.

Of the other victims, sadly, we know very little.

There were also a number of other men who narrowly escaped Nilsen's clutches in his home. There were men who, like Andrew Ho and Toshimitsu Ozawa, felt the tie around their necks and managed to run. There were men who awoke in a smoky room to find Nilsen 'rescuing' them.

There were also people who felt betrayed by Nilsen in a personal capacity. They had trusted him, worked with him, even befriended him. Some of them tried to contact him after his arrest, to express either support or disbelief, or anger.

On the 5th November 1983, Dennis Nilsen was sentenced to a minimum of 25 years in prison. The jury found him unanimously guilty on the count of the attempted murder of Paul Nobbs. Their decision was split 10-2 in favour of guilty on the other charges: the attempted murder of Douglas Stewart, and the murders of Kenneth Ockenden, Malcolm Barlow, Martyn Duffy, John Howlett, Billy Sutherland, and Stephen Sinclair. The other victims had not been identified at the time of his trial.

In 2006, changes to the law had Nilsen's hopes of parole quashed forever. He was told that he would never be eligible for it, and would never be released.

While I was researching the crimes, I wrote a letter to Nilsen, who was then still alive in prison. He died in May 2018, just before this book was released. I mentioned I was considering a novel, and asked for some insight into his life before it all started. He wrote back a letter full of pomp and false intelligence, designed to impress someone who doesn't understand long words, telling me not to bother.

That he disapproved, I felt, was a good enough reason to go ahead.

Made in the USA
Lexington, KY
12 December 2019